NE WEEK LOAN

D1424046

The Institute for Jewish Policy Research (JPR) is an independent think-tank that informs and influences policy, opinion and decision-making on social, political and cultural issues affecting Jewish life.
The Hate Debate is published as part of the JPR Civil Society programme, which includes research on antisemitism, racism and human rights.

Related JPR Civil Society publications

JPR Law Panel (Anthony Julius, Chair, Geoffrey Bindman, Jeffrey Jowell QC, Jonathan Morris, Dinah Rose and Malcolm Shaw)
Combating Holocaust denial through law in the United Kingdom
(2000)
David Capitanchik and Michael Whine
The governance of cyberspace: racism on the Internet
(1996)

THE HATE DEBATE
Should Hate Be Punished as a Crime?

Edited by
Paul Iganski

With essays by
Elizabeth Burney, Jeff Jacoby,
Valerie Jenness, Frederick M. Lawrence,
Jack Levin, Melanie Phillips, Larry Ray,
David Smith, Peter Tatchell

P

PROFILE BOOKS

jpr/

Institute for Jewish Policy Research

First published in 2002 by
Profile Books Ltd
58A Hatton Garden
London ECIN 8LX
www.profilebooks.co.uk

In association with
the Institute for Jewish Policy Research
79 Wimpole Street
London WIG 9RY
www.jpr.org.uk

An expanded version of the essay by Valerie Jenness (Chapter 2) is
published as 'The hate crime canon and beyond: a critical assessment',
Law and Critique, vol. 12, no. 3, 2001, 279–308

Typeset in Times by MacGuru
info@macguru.org.uk
Printed and bound in Great Britain by
Hobbs the Printers

A CIP catalogue record for this book is available from the British Library.

ISBN 1 86197 449 3

CONTENTS

NOTES ON CONTRIBUTORS

Elizabeth Burney is Senior Research Associate at Cambridge University's Institute of Criminology. During a varied research career she has published books on race and housing; lay magistrates; youth court sentencing; as well as a critique of social landlords' methods of controlling crime and disorder. Recently she completed research for the Home Office on the use of racially aggravated offences legislation. She is on the council of the Howard League for Penal Reform, a victim support volunteer and a Fellow of the Royal Society of Arts.

Paul Iganski is a lecturer in sociology and criminology at the University of Essex, England, and Civil Society Fellow at the Institute for Jewish Policy Research, London. He is also a visiting scholar at the Brudnick Center on Violence and Conflict at Northeastern University, Boston. He has carried out research and published articles on hate crime laws in the United States and Britain, racial stratification, and equal employment opportunity policies. He is co-author (with David

Mason) of *Ethnicity and Equality of Opportunity in the British National Health Service* (2002).

Jeff Jacoby is an award-winning columnist for the *Boston Globe*. His articles on hate and hate crimes include 'Why this death didn't count' (9 December 1999), '1999: The year in liberal hate speech' (30 December 1999), 'Banned in Boston' (6 April 2000) and 'Hate crimes laws send a terrible message' (22 June 2000).

Valerie Jenness is chair of the Department of Criminology, Law and Society and an associate professor at the University of California, Irvine. Her research focuses on the links between deviance and social control (especially law), gender, and social change (especially social movements). She is the author of three books: *Making Hate a Crime: From Social Movement to Law Enforcement Practice* (2001), *Hate Crimes: New Social Movements and the Politics of Violence* (1997) and *Making it Work: The Prostitutes' Rights Movement in Perspective* (1993). She has also published numerous articles on the politics of prostitution, AIDS and civil liberties, hate crimes and hate crime law, the gay/lesbian movement and the women's movement in the United States.

Frederick M. Lawrence is Law Alumni Scholar and Professor of Law at the Boston University School of Law. Previously he was an Assistant United States Attorney for the Southern District of New York and served as Chief of the Civil Rights

Unit of that office in the mid-1980s. Professor Lawrence was awarded an Inns of Court Fellowship in 1996 at the Institute for Advanced Legal Studies in London and a Ford Foundation Grant in 1998 and 1999 for the study of racially motivated crimes under British law, and during the spring 2001 semester was a Senior Honorary Research Fellow at University College London. He is the author of *Punishing Hate: Bias Crimes under American Law* (Harvard 1999).

Jack Levin is the Brudnick Professor of Sociology and Criminology at Northeastern University, Boston, where he directs the Brudnick Center on Violence and Conflict. He has written a number of books on hate and violence including *The Functions of Prejudice* (1982), *Hate Crimes: The Rising Tide of Bigotry and Bloodshed* (1993) and *The Violence of Hate: Confronting Racism, Anti-Semitism, and Other Forms of Bigotry* (2001).

Melanie Phillips is a social commentator whose columns have appeared in the *Guardian*, *Observer*, *Sunday Times* and now the *Daily Mail*. She is also the author of *All Must Have Prizes* (Warner), *The Sex-Change Society* (Social Market Foundation) and *America's Social Revolution* (Civitas). A selection of her writing can be found at www.melaniephillips.com.

Larry Ray is Professor of Sociology at the University of Kent, where he has worked since 1998. In addition to the research described in his article he has worked extensively on political reconstruction and problems of ethnicity and nationalism in post-Communist societies. He is currently working on a project examining experiences of harassment and support networks among ethnic minorities in the Canterbury area.

David Smith has been Professor of Social Work at Lancaster University since 1993. His research interests are criminology and criminal justice, and he often works with offenders. He has recently published the reports *Working with Persistent Juvenile Offenders* and *Witness Support in Scotland* for the Scottish Office. He is a former probation officer and uses criminological research to promote socially inclusive and re-integrative policies and practice with regard to offenders.

Peter Tatchell is a journalist, author, broadcaster and campaigner on gay and other human rights issues. For more than thirty years he has been confronting and shaming homophobic presidents, archbishops, police chiefs, generals and prime ministers. For more details, see his website (www.petertatchell.net).

THE HATE DEBATE

1

INTRODUCTION: THE PROBLEM OF HATE CRIMES AND HATE CRIME LAWS

Paul Iganski

S o-called 'hate crimes', or 'bias crimes', frequently make the headlines. The bombing in May 1999 of the Admiral Duncan, a 'gay pub' in Soho, London, in which three died and scores were injured; the callous attack on the young gay man Matthew Shepard who was pistol-whipped and left lashed to a fence in freezing conditions to die later in hospital in Wyoming in October 1998; the brutal murder by white supremacists of James Byrd, who was beaten unconscious, chained to the back of a pickup truck and dragged for miles along rural roads outside the town of Jasper, Texas in June 1998; and the racist murder of black teenager Stephen Lawrence in South London in 1993: these are some of the prominent hate crimes brought before the public eye by the media. But behind these well-publicized incidents are thousands upon thousands of hate crimes that don't make the news. The volume of incidents clearly shows that hate crimes are a serious social problem and an unfortunate by-product of diverse and mobile societies. The greater the diversity in a society, the greater the potential for such crimes.

How best to deal with hate crime offenders is also a problem. In the United States most states have laws that impose extra punishment for crimes that are motivated by hate, in excess of the usual punishment for the same crimes when motivated by other reasons. Yet such exemplary punishment has been controversial. Critics argue that it erodes a fundamental human right. It amounts to the punishment of ideas, improper thinking and opinions deemed abhorrent by government. Opponents of hate crime laws use the 'slippery slope' argument, alleging that the punishment of bigoted motives opens the door to the punishment of any out-of-favour motive.

However, supporters of hate crime laws argue that it is not opinion that is being punished, and therefore offenders' human rights are not violated. Extra punishment is meted out for the extra harms caused by hate crimes, compared with the same but otherwise motivated crimes. Hate crimes hurt the victims more, they say, and they also hurt people beyond the immediate victim. And greater punishment for greater harm is a central principle of criminal sentencing.

In stark contrast to the situation in the United States, where the issue has generated strong controversy, there has been little debate about the longest-standing British version of a hate crime law: the provisions against racially aggravated offences in the 1998 Crime and Disorder Act. That law allows more severe punishment of offences that are racially motivated as well as offences in which there is manifest racial hostility.

Britain has not yet gone as far in extending the coverage as those US states that punish offenders more severely when their crimes are motivated by prejudice against the sexual orientation, gender, disability, age or political affiliation of their victims. But British law appears to be moving in that direction.

In the wake of concern about assaults against Muslims in Britain following the terrorist attack on the World Trade Center, Britain's hate crime provisions were extended, under the 2001 Anti-Terrorism, Crime and Security Act, to cover religiously aggravated offences. These provisions addressed a loophole in British law, as Muslims are not recognized as a 'racial' group—as defined by the 1976 Race Relations Act[1]— and hence hate crimes committed against them without manifest racial motivation or hostility have been beyond the remit of provisions against racially aggravated offences. The new religiously aggravated offences crept in without opposition under cover of the controversy over government plans—subsequently suspended—to establish provisions against incitement to religious hatred. Critics of hate crime laws in the United States would no doubt argue that Britain has slid further down the slippery slope of the punishment of thought.

How can we understand the emergence and extension of hate crime laws in the United States and in Britain? Do hate crime laws really create 'thought crimes'? Do they punish articulated ideas and opinions? Is extra punishment the most appropriate way to deal with offenders motivated by hate?

These are the questions that are debated in the following collection of essays, a unique gathering of divergent and, in some cases, competing opinions. The volume combines scholarship and polemic, not normally brought together in the same publication, by leading commentators in the United States and Britain drawn from the fields of civil rights activism, criminology, journalism and law.

In bringing out *The Hate Debate*, the Institute for Jewish Policy Research (JPR) is aiming not to promote any particular perspective. Instead it hopes to provide, as part of its Civil Society Programme, a plurality of opinion and analysis that could inform public policy debates on both sides of the Atlantic. Judging from the number of articles in the press, scholarly journals and even websites on the topic, the desirability of hate crime laws continues to be a highly controversial subject in the United States. But the debate seems to have reached a stalemate between opponents and supporters of the laws. *The Hate Debate* offers some new thinking to take that debate forward. It also aims to generate much-needed debate in Britain, where there has mostly been silence about the question of punishing hate—despite strong support for protecting freedom of expression, evident in the recent controversy over government proposals to create an offence of incitement to religious hatred.

The problem of hate crime

How serious is the problem of hate crime? It would be useful to open the hate debate by examining the scale of the problem that hate crime laws address. But finding reliable data is a problem in itself. It is well known that official crime statistics understate the true extent of criminal behaviour. Hate crime statistics are no exception. In the United States, under the Hate Crime Data Collection Program, law enforcement agencies voluntarily submit data about hate crimes within their jurisdiction to the FBI's Uniform Crime Reporting Program. But, according to the Southern Poverty Law Center's *Intelligence Report* (winter 2001) and research commissioned by the US Bureau of Justice Assistance,[2] the reporting system is full of gaping holes. Not all crimes are reported, and not all law enforcement agencies submit data. The Southern Poverty Law Center estimates the number of hate crimes to be six times greater than the number reported by the FBI.

Over half of the hate crimes recorded in the FBI's data for the year 2000 involved victims targeted because of their race, ethnicity or national origin, and they included sixteen murders. Police data on racist incidents in England and Wales show a much higher number of incidents than the FBI data. But a transatlantic comparison is fraught with danger. The criteria used by the FBI for defining hate crimes are far more stringent than those used by police services in England and Wales. For an incident to be reported as a hate crime by the FBI, there must be *sufficient objective facts ... to lead a reasonable and prudent person to conclude that the offender's actions were motivated, in whole or in part, by bias*.[3] Police services in England and Wales collect data on racist incidents defined more broadly, as recommended by the Stephen Lawrence

Table 1 **Hate crime incidents by bias motivation**

Race	**4,337**
Anti-White	875
Anti-Black	2,884
Anti-American Indian/Alaskan native	57
Anti-Asian/Pacific Islander	281
Anti-multiracial group	240
Religion	**1,472**
Anti-Jewish	1,109
Anti-Catholic	56
Anti-Protestant	59
Anti-Islamic	28
Anti-other religious group	172
Anti-multireligious group	44
Anti-atheism/agnosticism/etc	4
Sexual Orientation	**1,299**
Anti-male homosexual	896
Anti-female homosexual	179
Anti-homosexual	182
Anti-heterosexual	22
Anti-bisexual	20
Ethnicity/national origin	**911**
Anti-Hispanic	557
Anti-other ethnicity/national origin	354
Disability	**36**
Anti-physical	20
Anti-mental	16
Multiple-bias incidents	**8**
Total	**8,063**

Source: US Department of Justice, Federal Bureau of Investigation, Uniform Crime Reports, *Hate Crime Statistics 2000* (www.fbi.gov/ucr/cius_00/hate00.pdf)

Inquiry,[4] to include *any incident which is perceived to be racist by the victim or any other person.* Recorded incidents don't even have to be identifiable offences. But even these data understate the true extent of the problem.

The British Crime Survey, which annually asks a random sample of the British population about their experiences of crime, has shown that the estimated number of incidents considered by victims to be racially motivated far exceeds the number recorded by the police. For 1999 the British Crime Survey estimated nearly six times as many racially motivated incidents as reported in the police statistics. It also clearly indicates the scale of the problem: racially motivated incidents accounted for one in forty of *all* crimes.

The problem of racially motivated crime was even worse in the mid-1990s. It is well known that crime statistics can misrepresent criminal trends. Again, hate crime statistics are no exception. Racist incidents recorded by police forces in England and Wales have shown a year on year rise. But the pattern may reflect changes in police recording practices and a greater motivation by victims to report crimes, as the British Crime Survey indicates a decline in racist incidents across the late 1990s.

The FBI data show that significant numbers of hate crime victims are targeted because of their religion or their sexual orientation. There are no equivalent official data for Britain. But in a poll of British Muslims by BBC Radio's news programme *Today*, conducted between 2 and 11 November, in the aftermath of the destruction of the World Trade Center, 30 per cent of respondents reported perceived hostility or abuse

7

Figure 1 **Racist incidents for all police force areas in England and Wales**

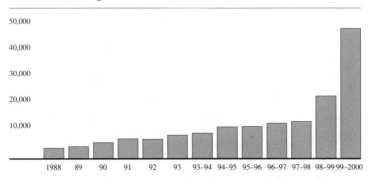

Sources: 1988 to 1996–7 data taken from *Racial Violence and Harassment. A Consultation Document*, London: Home Office 1997 (www.homeoffice.gov.uk.rvah.htm) 1997–8 to 1999–2000 data taken from *Statistics on Race and the Criminal Justice System*, London: Home Office 2000 (www.homeoffice.gov.uk/rds/pdfs/s95raceopdf)

---

towards them, or a member of their family, from non-Muslims as a result of the events on September 11th.[5] Although it cannot be determined how much of the hostility was manifested as crime. Furthermore, as Peter Tatchell says in his contribution, surveys in Britain have shown that large proportions of lesbian women and gay men have been victims of homophobic hate crimes.

The problem of hate crime laws

Is it just for offenders who commit a violent assault because of prejudice against their victim to be punished more severely than other offenders who commit the same assault just for the hell of it? Take two people, both beaten bloody, lying on the

Figure 2 **Estimates from the 1995 and 1999 British Crime Surveys of the number of incidents considered by the victim to be racially motivated**

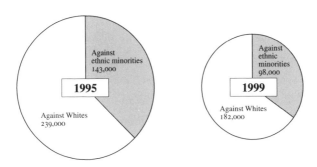

Sources: *Statistics on Race and the Criminal Justice System*, London: Home Office 2000, Chapter 8: 'Racial incidents and crimes'

ground. Tell one of them: 'We're going to take the crime against you less seriously than the crime against the person next to you because of what was in the mind of his attacker.' Many people would find such an idea offensive. But that is the principle behind hate crime laws in the United States and in Britain.

Opponents argue that hate crime laws provide extra punishment for bad values. As Melanie Phillips argues in her essay, provisions for racially and religiously aggravated offences in Britain proscribe 'certain attitudes of mind'. Furthermore, as Jeff Jacoby argues in his, hate crime laws create an 'indefensible double-standard' by proclaiming that hurting some 'kinds of people' isn't quite as bad as hurting others.

However, supporters of hate crime laws argue that they are not advocating the punishment of expression, the thought behind the crime or the motivation. Instead, they support greater punishment for the greater harms allegedly inflicted by hate crimes. Those harms make hate crimes qualitatively different from the same crimes motivated by other reasons. From this perspective the motives or the words of the perpetrator are only relevant as an indicator of the type of act committed, not as the basis for punishment.

In his essay Frederick Lawrence argues that hate crimes hurt more than parallel, otherwise motivated, crimes. This notion has firmly taken root in the defence of hate crime laws. It has been highly influential and was a key argument in the landmark case of *Wisconsin* v. *Mitchell* (113 S. Ct. at 2201 [1993]) that settled the constitutional questions about hate crime laws in the United States.

But how do hate crimes hurt more? Exactly what is the nature of the harms inflicted? I address these questions in my essay, arguing that there are few circumstances in which the harms allegedly inflicted by hate crimes don't amount to revulsion at the offender's motivations. Should supporters of hate crime laws then stand by their principles and honestly declare that their objective is to punish offenders for their bad values, values incongruent with civil society?

There are other important questions addressed by *The Hate Debate*. Not all states in the US have enacted hate crime laws that cover all the categories of victims included in the FBI's hate crime statistics. Similarly in Britain, hate crimes in which victims are singled out because of their sexual orientation, for instance, are not subject to the same legislative provisions that

Crime and Disorder Act 1998

Racially-aggravated offences: England and Wales
Section 28. An offence is racially aggravated if
(a) at the time of committing the offence, or immediately before or after doing so, the offender demonstrates towards the victim of the offence hostility based on the victim's membership (or presumed membership) of a racial group; or
(b) the offence is motivated (wholly or partly) by hostility towards members of a racial group based on their membership of that group.

Penalty enhancements first established by the Act for racially aggravated offences:

Existing offence	Maximum penalty for basic offence	Maximum penalty for racially aggravated offence
Common assault	6 months and/or a level 5 fine (£5,000)	2 years imprisonment and/or an unlimited fine
Assault occasioning actual bodily harm	5 years imprisonment	7 years imprisonment
Malicious wounding	5 years imprisonment	7 years imprisonment
Criminal damage (section 1(1) Criminal Damage Act 1971)	10 years imprisonment	14 years imprisonment
Section 5 Public Order Act 1986: disorderly behaviour	Level 3 fine (£1,000)	Level 4 fine (£2,500)
S. 4A Public Order Act 1986: intentional harassment	6 months and/or a level 5 fine (£5,000)	2 years and/or an unlimited fine
S. 4 Public Order Act 1986: threatening behaviour	6 months and/or a level 5 fine (£5,000)	2 years and/or an unlimited fine
S. 2 Protection from Harassment Act 1997: harassment	6 months and/or a level 5 fine (£5,000)	2 years and/or an unlimited fine
S. 4 Protection from Harassment Act 1997: fear of violence	5 years and/or an unlimited fine	7 years and/or an unlimited fine

As amended by the Anti-Terrorism, Crime and Security Act 2001 (Section 39)
An offence is racially or religiously aggravated if
(a) at the time of committing the offence, or immediately before or after doing so, the offender demonstrates towards the victim of the offence hostility based on the victim's membership (or presumed membership) of a racial group or religious group; or
(b) the offence is motivated (wholly or partly) by hostility towards members of a racial or religious group based on their membership of that group.
In this section 'religious group' means a group of persons defined by reference to religious belief or lack of religious belief.

apply to racially and religiously aggravated crimes. By such omissions, don't hate crime laws create new injustices? Once established, shouldn't the law be broadened, as Peter Tatchell argues in his contribution, to encompass hate crimes affecting all vulnerable communities? Yet such logic does not necessarily win the argument for legislation. As Valerie Jenness shows in her essay, the enactment of hate crime law is contingent upon the interplay between social movement activism, political expediency, prevailing legal culture and the impact of critical events, as well as arguments for social justice.

The question of the value of punishment, as against other interventions, for hate crime offences is also addressed by *The Hate Debate*. Jack Levin, in his contribution, observes that the great majority of hate crimes are committed not by members of organized hate groups, but by those he calls 'dabblers in hate'. Furthermore, he argues that the actions of perpetrators are sanctioned by others in the wider community who sympathize with bigotry, and also by those who are passive bystanders in the face of its demonstration. This raises questions about the appropriate ways of tackling hate. Similarly, Larry Ray and David Smith argue in their essay, which draws on research into convicted perpetrators of racist crimes, that such crimes are best understood not by focusing on the intent or the motives of offenders, but by examining the cultures of racism and violence within which racist offending takes place.

In acknowledging the social context in which hate crimes are committed, it is important to ask, as Elizabeth Burney does, whether the courts are always the right place for dealing with hate crimes? Prosecution, in Elizabeth Burney's view, should be part of a varied, holistic and vigorous policy of confronting bigotry that, in her words, 'is appropriate to the situation and feelings of the victim'. Are the courts, then, the right place for dealing with hate?

Notes

1   See Sukhwinder S. Chokar and Kuljeet S. Dobe, 'Muslims, ethnicity and the law', *International Journal of Discrimination and the Law*, vol. 4, 2000, 369–86.

2   Center for Criminal Justice Policy Research, College of Criminal Justice, Northeastern University, Boston, and the Justice Research and Statistics Association, Washington, DC, *Improving the Quality and Accuracy of Bias Crime Statistics Nationally, An Assessment of the First Ten Years of Bias Crime Data Collection*, report submitted to the Bureau of Justice Statistics, US Department of Justice, September 2000 (www.dac.neu.edu/cj).

3   Federal Bureau of Investigation, *Hate Crime Data Collection Guidelines*, Washington, DC: Federal Bureau of Investigation, US Department of Justice 1999, 4–6 (www.fbi.gov/ucr/hatecrime.pdf).

4   Sir William Macpherson, *The Stephen Lawrence Inquiry: Report of an Inquiry by Sir William Macpherson of Cluny* (Cm 4262-1), London: The Stationery Office, 1999, recommendations 12–14, 328–9.

5   Robert Aitken, 'British Muslims oppose military action'
     (www.bbc.co.uk/radio4/today/reports/features/muslimpoll.
     html).

2

CONTOURS OF HATE CRIME POLITICS AND LAW IN THE UNITED STATES

Valerie Jenness

'Ay carumba. Hate crimes against capitalism!' So said Ryken Grattet, a leading expert on hate crime, after hearing about a new bill introduced in Portland, Oregon. Sponsored by State Senator Gary George (R-Newberg), the bill calls for an additional five years in prison for an offender whose crime is motivated by 'a hatred of people who subscribe to a set of political beliefs that support capitalism and the needs of people with respect to their balance with nature'.[1] If passed, according to the local press, this legislation would 'expand the definition of hate crimes in a novel direction: to include the actions of eco-terrorists and critics of capitalism'.[2] As interpreted by the national media, the bill would 'make it a hate crime to smash a Starbucks window or sabotage a timber company'.[3] Although the bill would expand Oregon's current hate crime law to include eco-terrorists and anti-capitalists, Senator George says his real target is 'political correctness'.

The Senator's motivation for introducing this national news-making proposal confirms the fact that the concept of 'hate crime' has been institutionalized in social, political and legislative discourse in the United States. Moreover, it signals the way in which hate crime discourse has invited the emergence of a counter-discourse and oppositional politics. In contrast, Grattet's reaction to the bill speaks to the way in which hate crime discourse has taken an arguably ironic turn, thus revealing the contradictions in, and points of contention over, the use of the term 'hate crime' to direct social and legal attention to violence against some types of victims and not others.

Although it remains an empirical question whether the United States is experiencing greater levels of hate- or bias-motivated conduct than in the past, it is beyond dispute that the concept of 'hate crime' has found a home in the US social and legal lexicon; as a result, the idea that criminal conduct is somehow different when it involves an act motivated by (some types of) bigotry, hatred or bias and manifested as discrimination against (some) minorities is increasingly accepted. But why now? Where did the concept 'hate crime' come from? How has it been institutionalized? And with what consequences? This essay addresses these historic changes by focusing on the relationship between 'hate crime' as a social and legal turn and American culture, identity politics and law. What, for example, has hate crime law meant for how violence is both signified and subject to social control in the modern era? What have these changes meant for minority communities implicated in hate crime discourse, as well as those who have gone unnoticed? And what does all of this say about 'the hate debate', the theme of this book?

The emergence of 'hate crime' discourse in the United States

In the United States the use of the term 'hate crime' is now commonplace in settings as diverse as the evening news, academic conferences, legislative bodies, presidential proclamations and private conversations. From the introduction and politicization of the term in the late 1970s to the continued enforcement of hate crime law at the beginning of the twenty-first century, modern social movements have constructed the problem of bias-motivated violence in particular ways: politicians at both the federal and state level have made legislation that defines the parameters of hate crime; judicial decision-makers have elaborated and enriched the meaning of hate crime as they have grappled with questions about the constitutionality of 'hate crime' as a legal concept (Phillips and Grattet 2000); and law enforcement officials have continued to investigate, classify and prosecute bias-motivated incidents that may or may not be deemed hate crimes.

The emergence, circulation and institutionalization of the term 'hate crime' in both the legal and social lexicon signal an increasing acceptance of the idea that criminal conduct is somehow different when it involves an act motivated by bigotry and manifested as discrimination. Moreover, these developments signal that some types of victims of violence are worthy of additional, or at least uniquely delineated, public and legal concern. And, finally, they legitimate state sanctions against a newly signified category of perpetrators of crime. These changes are intimately connected to, if not explicitly derived from, the ways in which 'hate crime', as a modern and indigenous social fact, has been constructed across multiple institutional spheres of social life in the United States (Jenness and Grattet 2001).

As a political and legal concept, 'hate crime' was first developed and promulgated by diverse social movements and subsequently defined and institutionalized by state and federal lawmakers. It finally passed constitutional muster in the US appellate courts and thus continues to be applied—to a greater or lesser degree—by law enforcement officials. By the 1990s 'hate crime' had found a home in the most visible venues of national policy discourse in the United States. For example, in his 1990 State of the Union message, President Bush urged Americans: 'Everyone of us must confront and condemn racism, Anti-Semitism, bigotry and hate. Not next week, not tomorrow, but right now.'[4] This declaration was later underscored by John Conyers, Jr. (D-Michigan), a member of the US House of Representatives: 'whether based on sexual orientation, race, religion, or ethnicity, bigotry and the violence it inspires pose a grave threat to the peace and harmony of our communities. The need to alert Americans to this threat is great' (US Congress 1992:xv).

These comments, and many others like them, certify 'hate crime' as a socially recognized category of behaviour, a legal concept and a social problem worthy of public concern and collective action. With this socio-legal development in mind, it is useful and timely to ask: how did the United States get to this point, especially in light of the fact that violence organized around axes of social differentiation—such as race, religion, ethnicity, nationality, national origin, sexuality, gender, (dis)abilities and so on—is not particularly new and arguably in decline (Jacobs and Potter 1998)?

Social movements and the creation of a 'hate crime' issue in the United States

In the United States the idea of hate crime emerged through the confluence of several social movement discourses, most notably the black civil rights movement, the women's movement, the gay and lesbian movement, the disabilities rights movement and the crime victim movement. These movements converged to form the modern anti-hate crime movement, which in turn proved crucial to the development of US hate crime law. Although they differ in extremely important ways, historically these movements have shared a common commitment to publicizing, framing and combating violence directed at minorities *because of* their minority status.

Prior to the invention and institutionalization of the term 'hate crime', the modern civil rights movement politicized violence against racial minorities, such as police brutality against Blacks; the women's movement politicized violence against women, including rape and domestic violence; the gay and lesbian movement politicized violence against homosexuals, especially 'gay bashing'; and the disabilities rights movement politicized violence against persons with disabilities, such as the so-called 'mercy killings' of those deemed unfit to live meaningful lives. As these civil rights movements sought to expand legal, economic, educational and social opportunities for select minority constituencies, they sponsored anti-violence projects to combat discriminatory violence directed at racial/ethnic, gendered, sexual and (dis)abilities-based constituencies (Goldberg 1991). Developed prior to the emergence of a hate crime discourse in the United States, these anti-violence projects disseminated a commonly expressed theme: violence is not merely epiphenomenal to the various systems of discrimination but, rather, central to their maintenance.

The themes emerging from a considerably less progressive social movement in the United States, the crime victim movement, also set the stage for the emergence of hate crime discourse. Typically deemed a conservative campaign, the crime victim movement is comprised of a fairly diverse range of groups, including some of the civil rights groups mentioned above, committed to putting forth a basic grievance: victims of crime, especially violent crime, not only need but are entitled to special assistance, support and rights *as crime victims*. From the point of view of those involved in the crime victim movement, 'the criminal justice system was not perceived as providing certainty of justice for the criminal or the victim' (Weed 1995:21). Thus, advocates for victims' rights argue that legal and extra-legal mechanisms are needed to recognize and serve those injured by crime, especially violent crime. One result of this advocacy has been the passage of a 'crime victim bill of rights' in almost every state in the union (Weed 1995).

The anti-hate crime movement emerged out of a fusion of the strategies and goals of several identifiable precursor movements that laid the foundation upon which the new movement could question, and make publicly debatable, issues of 'rights' and 'harm' as they relate to a variety of constituencies. One of the major achievements of the anti-hate crime movement is that it unites disparate social movements, what some would refer to as 'strange bedfellows'. As liberal, progressive movements, the civil rights, women's, disabilities rights, and gay and lesbian movements 'called attention to the personal costs of minority groups' political victimization', while the more conservative crime victim movement 'called attention to the political context of personal victimization' (Maroney 1998:579).

With its complicated and sometimes contradictory political forces in place, the anti-hate crime movement in the United States invented the term 'hate crime', defined its initial properties and demanded that lawmakers and other public policy officials recognize bias-motivated violence as a significant social problem. Interestingly, however, at least early on, it did so without the official backing of the state; that is, the term 'hate crime' was popularly used by these movements and the media prior to state and federal lawmakers bestowing it with legal authority via the passage of statutes. Thereafter, throughout the 1980s and 1990s, the players described above were successful at getting social movement goals translated into public policy, namely, state and federal law.

Extending the reach of the state

In *Hate Crimes: Criminal Law and Identity Politics* (1998), James B. Jacobs and Kimberly Potter offer a scathing critique of hate crime politics and law. They do so by first refuting two interrelated notions promulgated by these social movement players: first, that bias-motivated violence is occurring with alarming frequency and, second, that its rate of occurrence is also increasing alarmingly. Rejecting these widely held notions, James B. Jacobs and Jessica Henry argue that the 'rising tide of bigotry and bloodshed' described by Jack Levin and Jack McDevitt in 1993, as well as by many others, is a social construction that evidences a modern moral panic (Jacobs and Henry 1996). According to Jacobs and Potter,

> *the passage of hate crime law in the 1980s and 1990s is best explained by the growing influence of identity politics. Fundamentally, hate crime laws are symbolic statements requested by advocacy groups for material and symbolic reasons and provided by politicians for political reasons (Jacobs and Potter 1998:65).*

Taking identity politics as the engine that drives hate crime as a social and legal concept, critics like Jacobs and Potter argue that hate crime laws are a vivid example of legislators ceding the policymaking process to interest groups. In simple terms, what begins as a social movement goal ends as official state policy. With this causal analysis in hand, critics like Jacobs warn against the marriage of symbolic politics and official state policy, arguing that such a marriage represents a misuse of criminal law in modern democratic societies.

But simple terms and accordant variables—like 'identity politics' and 'interest group politics'—very rarely capture the whole story of legal reform or any other type of policy innovation, diffusion and implementation; rather, they belie more complex political processes that predict not only the timing of the passage of laws and other forms of public policy, but also the content and implementation of such laws and policies. A growing body of research suggests that a range of factors are at issue, including a diverse array of social actors, interest groups, social movements, political opportunities and structural conditions. Interest groups are only part of the reason that hate crime politics, discourse and law emerged when and how they did, and why they took root in the way they have. The ways activists, experts and policymakers have conceptualized and drafted hate crime legislation reflects the constraints and opportunities of using the law, as opposed to other institutions, to address systemic conflicts and inequalities. Most notably, legal culture in the United States has affected how interests have been expressed and consequently how laws and their surrounding discourse have been formulated.

One key element of law in the United States that significantly shaped the formulation of hate crime legislation is the 'norm of sameness'. As a basic assumption of American law and thus lawmaking, the 'norm of sameness' is best expressed in the equal protection clause of the US Constitution and is echoed in innumerable other locations. Simply put, the 'norm of sameness' stipulates that laws must apply equally to all groups and individuals in society. As a journalist observed with regard to hate crime, 'a large stone in the foundation of the American dream is the idea that every person is equal in citizenship and that every life should be equally valued and protected. No one should accept less, but is anyone entitled to more?' (Dickey 2000:29). For the most part, 'equal' treatment historically has meant 'sameness': that is, a law must not give one group benefits or protections that it does not extend to others. All groups must be treated the same (Minow 1990). The norm of sameness is so pervasive in US law that it inevitably structures the way interest groups and policymakers orient themselves in relation to emergent problems.

In the case of hate crime, the norm of sameness ensures that terms like 'race', 'religion' and 'gender', instead of 'Blacks', 'Jews' and 'women', anchor various formulations of hate crime law and attendant discourse. Hate crime laws are written in a way that elides the historical basis and meaning of such crimes by translating specific categories of persons (such as Blacks, Jews, gays and lesbians, Mexicans etc.) into all-encompassing and seemingly neutral categories (such as race, religion, sexual orientation and national origin). In doing so, the laws do not offer these groups any remedies or protections that are not simultaneously available to all other races, religions, genders, sexual orientations, nationalities and so on. Minorities are treated the same as their counterparts.

The result is significant: in order to ensure that lawmakers do not give to particular groups benefits that are not also extended to all others (Lawrence 1999), the policymaking process changed the meaning that activists originally attached to the concept of a hate crime. Most notably, sameness in the context of hate crime has meant that laws have been written in a way that equates a hate crime against a Black with one against a White, ensuring 'within-category sameness'. This was not the intent of the civil rights movements. Similarly, hate crimes against persons with disabilities are rendered equivalent to hate crimes against Muslims, ensuring 'across-category sameness'. Again, this was not the intent of the civil rights movements. The institutionalization of 'within-category sameness' and 'across-category sameness' results in a clear disconnection between the origins of hate crime politics, the development of hate crime policy (that is, legislation) and the implementation of that policy (that is, law enforcement).

At the end of the day, the identity politics that invented hate crime discourse and fuelled the development of hate crime law in the United States are inevitably muted as the mandates of American law and policymaking are addressed. Therefore, to attribute the complex process of policymaking to one variable—interest group politics—is myopic at best and grossly misleading at worst. In this case, to envision hate crime law as 'merely' derivative of modern identity politics is misguided. If hate crime law represents a marriage between identity politics and the state, it is a marriage that refuses to acknowledge a complicated courtship, many break-ups and make-ups, the number of diverse guests at the wedding, continuing adulterous affairs and, most importantly, the ongoing potential for divorce. Although it is difficult to argue against the notion that identity politics inspired the development of hate crime discourse in the United States, it is equally difficult to conclude that identity politics is the beginning and the endpoint of the development of hate crime law.

Status provisions: signifying 'victims'

Another key feature of US hate crime law—'status provisions', or what Sarah Soule and Jennifer Earl (1999) refer to as 'target groups'—also deserves critical assessment. Status provisions single out some axes of oppression as part and parcel of the hate crime problem in the United States, while rendering invisible other axes around which violence is organized. One of the most important elements of the substantive character of hate crime law—the adoption of select status provisions, such as race, religion, ethnicity, sexual orientation, gender and disabilities—ensured that *some* victims of discriminatory violence have been acknowledged as hate crime victims while others have gone unnoticed. In particular, people of colour, Jews, gays and lesbians, women and those with disabilities increasingly have been recognized as victims of hate crime, while members of trade unions, octogenarians, the elderly, children and police officers, for example, have not. In short, some groups that are differentially vulnerable to crime have been deemed victims worthy of legal redress, and some have not.

In 1988 Representative John Conyers, Jr., the federal legislator most responsible for holding federal hearings on hate crime in the United States, proclaimed that 'hate crimes motivated by intolerance need to be distinguished from other crimes motivated by other factors' (US Congress 1988:8). But, at the time, which types of distinctions should be written into law was an open question. And it remains an open question. Early on, the anti-hate crime social movement highlighted some types of victims; as the hate crime concept entered the legislative arena, its possibilities and limits remained unclear. Citizens, activists and policymakers alike continue to ask: who else might it be relevant to include?

It is instructive to compare the status provisions included in hate crime laws in 1988 and 1998, ten and twenty years, respectively, after the first state hate crime law was passed. In 1988 the most common status provisions were for race, religion, colour and national origin. This set of status provisions is associated with the most visible, recognizable and stereotypical kinds of discriminatory behaviour in US history and contemporary society, such as, for example, violence towards or harassment of Blacks, immigrants and Jews. While other provisions—such as gender, ancestry, sexual orientation, creed, age, political affiliation and marital status—are recognized in the early development of hate crime discourse and attendant law, they appear infrequently. These provisions were not part of legislators' original conception of the 'normal' axes along which hate crimes occur. By 1998, however, a second tier of categories had clearly emerged, with sexual orientation, gender and disability becoming increasingly recognized in state hate crime law, a pattern that was replicated at the federal level. While less stereotypical than their pre-decessors, especially early on in the development of hate crime law and discourse, these status markers have become increasingly recognized as axes along which hate-motivated violence, and thus hate crime, occur.

The respective unfolding of these clusters of statuses—the core and the second tier—reflect the history of various post-1960s civil rights movements in the United States. Race, religion, colour and national origin reflect the early legal contestation of minorities' status and rights. Thus, there is a more developed history of invoking and then deploying the law, especially civil rights law, to protect and enhance the status of Blacks, Jews and immigrants. In contrast, the gay and lesbian movement, the women's movement and the disabilities rights movement reflect a 'second wave' of civil rights activism and 'identity politics' (Goldberg 1991) in the United States. Accordingly, sexual orientation, gender and disability have only recently been recognized in US hate crime law. As evidenced by US congressional hearings on hate crime, these are also more heavily contested protected statuses than the 'first wave' categories (Jenness 1999). Not surprisingly, they remain less embedded in hate crime law. Finally, marital status, creed, age, membership in the armed service, and political affiliation are not visibly connected to issues of discrimination and victimization by any particular mass movement, and are fairly anomalous provisions in US hate crime law.

Moving well beyond these rare provisions, an array of new-found provisions are emerging. For example, recall the anti-capitalism provision discussed in the opening paragraph of this essay. Although it is not a commonly proposed provision, it is nonetheless an innovative one that is attracting national attention. Similarly, states have proposed legislation that would define one's position on the abortion debate as a basis for hate crime victimization. California State Senator Deborah Ortiz (D-6th District), for example, is sponsoring a measure that would 'increase penalties for crime committed against those exercising their freedom of reproductive choice to match penalties for committing crimes classified as hate crimes' (DeGiere 2001:5).

Borrowing from the social problems literature, this process of extending the reach of hate crime law can be described as 'domain expansion'. Domain expansion occurs when claims-makers of all sorts—activists, policymakers, legal scholars and other academics, the media and so on—offer new definitions of the phenomenon being deemed problematic. As a result, the boundaries of that phenomenon are expanded and the amount of substantive territory falling under the rubric of the social problem—in this case, hate crime—increases over time. Clearly, this is a central feature of the development of hate crime law. However, domain expansion is not unique to the problem of hate crime.[5]

Developing contours of hate crime politics and law

It is beyond dispute that American history, and indeed world history, is replete with violence organized around markers of social differentiation, such as race, ethnicity, nationality, religion, gender, sexual orientation, age, ability, political beliefs and affiliations, and so on. What is new and interesting about such violence is the way in which it has been redefined as 'hate crime' in the United States and, increasingly, elsewhere. The emergence, circulation and institutionalization of the term 'hate crime' in the social, legal and policy lexicon signal an increasing acceptance of the idea that bias-motivated conduct manifested as systematic discrimination is a social problem.

This formulation of 'the hate crime problem' is intimately connected to contemporary crime control efforts in the United States, the development of civil and criminal law, the allocation of civil rights (to some and not others), and the symbolic status of (select) minorities. As with all social facts, especially those falling within the legal domain, hate crime is a contingent and ongoing construction that reflects the outgrowth of the interplay between social movement activism, policymakers, legal culture and the meanings they engender. In addition, a number of social structures and social processes have been, and continue to be, crucial in the development of US hate crime discourse. Most notably, the 'loosely coupled' political structure and criminal justice system (Hagan 1989) and the process of domain expansion (Best 1990, Jenness 1995) have been consequential for the development of US hate crime law.

With regard to social structure, the loose coupling of the various institutional spheres that have contributed to the invention, development and institutionalization of US hate crime discourse is significant. Specifically, the nature of the relationship between the social movement activists who invented and continue to promote the social problem of hate-motivated violence, the lawmakers who enact hate crime law that defines the parameters of hate *crime* (proper), the appellate court judges who fix more elaborate and complicated meanings to select elements of hate crime law (such as 'the intent standard'), and the law enforcement officials has ensured that the content, structure and workings of hate crime discourse have changed over time. Often this has occurred with unpredictable consequences, most notably the ongoing disconnection between activists' political intentions (that is, to combat bigotry) and the content and working of hate crime policy (that is, to give all 'equal protection').

As for significant social processes, American legal culture coupled with domain expansion has led to the emergence of strange bedfellows: violence against Blacks is rendered equivalent to violence against Asians in so far as both are racialized groups; violence organized around 'race' or 'ethnicity' is rendered equivalent to violence organized around gender or disability in so far as both constitute legitimate status provisions; violence against Christians is equivalent to violence against Jews in so far as both fall under the 'religion' provision of hate crime law; contemporary lynchers now share discursive space with anti-capitalists in so far as both are part of the hate crime discourse; and, finally, it has become reasonable to talk about violence against any person because they associate/d with someone targeted because of *any* social category as a hate crime. These outcomes represent just a few of the arguably unanticipated contours of hate crime politics and hate crime law in the United States.

Notes

1 'Senator questions laws against hate crimes', *The Oregonian*, 10 February 2001, D01.
2 Ibid.
3 'Legislator seeks to expand hate crime laws, sort of', Associated Press, 10 February 2001.
4 *New York Times*, 1 February 1990, D22.
5 See, for example, Joel Best's work on domain expansion and its applicability to child abuse law in the United States (Best 1990).

References

Best, Joel (1990), *Threatened Children: Rhetoric and Concern about Child Victims*, Chicago: University of Chicago Press.

DeGiere, Gregory (2001), 'Crimes against reproductive rights in California', Senate Office of Research Report 1088-S (May), California State Senate, Sacramento, CA: Senate Publications (an updated version is available on-line: www.sen.ca.gov/sor).

Dickey, Fred (2000), 'Of course hate crimes are wrong: but so are the laws against them', *Los Angeles Times Magazine*, 22 October, 10–29.

Goldberg, Robert A. (1991), *Grassroots Resistance: Social Movements in the Twentieth Century*, Belmont, CA: Wadsworth Publishing.

Hagan, John (1989), 'Why is there so little criminal justice theory? Neglected macro- and microlevel links between organization and power', *Journal of Research in Crime and Delinquency*, vol. 26, 116–35.

Jacobs, James B. and Kimberly Potter (1998), *Hate Crimes: Criminal Law and Identity Politics*, New York: Oxford University Press.

Jacobs, James B. and Jessica S. Henry (1996), 'The social construction of a hate crime epidemic', *Journal of Criminal Law and Criminology*, vol. 86, no. 2, 366–91.

Jenness, Valerie (1995), 'Social movement growth, domain expansion, and framing processes: the gay/lesbian

movement and violence against gays and lesbians as a
social problem', *Social Problems*, vol. 42, 145–70.

——— (1999), 'Managing differences and making
legislation: social movements and the racialization,
sexualization, and gendering of federal hate crime law in
the U.S., 1985–1998', *Social Problems*, vol. 46, 548–71.

——— and Ryken Grattet (2001), *Making Hate a Crime:
From Social Movement to Law Enforcement*, New York:
Russell Sage.

Lawrence, Frederick M. (1999), *Punishing Hate: Bias Crimes
under American Law*, Cambridge, MA: Harvard
University Press.

Levin, Jack and Jack McDevitt (1993), *Hate Crimes: The Rising
Tide of Bigotry and Bloodshed*, New York: Plenum Press.

Maroney, Terry A. (1998), 'The struggle against hate crime:
movement at a crossroads', *New York University Law
Review*, vol. 73, 564–620.

Minow, Martha (1990), *Making All the Difference: Inclusion,
Exclusion, and American Law*, Ithaca, NY: Cornell
University Press.

Phillips, Scott and Ryken Grattet (2000), 'Judicial rhetoric,
meaning-making, and the institutionalization of hate
crime law', *Law and Society Review*, vol. 34, 567–606.

Soule, Sarah and Jennifer Earl (1999), 'All men are created
equal: the differential protection of minority groups in hate
crime legislation', paper presented at the annual meeting
of the American Sociological Association, Chicago.

US Congress (1988), 'Racially-Motivated Violence',

Hearings before the Subcommittee on Criminal Justice of the Committee on the Judiciary, 100th Cong., 2nd sess., 11 May and 12 July, Serial 144, Washington, DC: Government Printing Office.

——— (1992), 'Hate Crimes Sentencing Enhancement Act of 1992', *Hearing before the Subcommittee on the Constitution of the Committee on the Judiciary*, 102nd Cong., 2nd sess., 5 August, Serial 42, Washington, DC: Government Printing Office.

Weed, Frank (1995), *Certainty of Justice: Reform in the Crime Victim Movement*, New York: Aldine.

3

RACIAL VIOLENCE ON A 'SMALL ISLAND': BIAS CRIME IN A MULTICULTURAL SOCIETY[1]

Frederick M. Lawrence

For the past several years, I have been involved in a study of racially motivated violence in Great Britain and its treatment under British law. A major component of this study is a comparison of British bias crime law with United States bias crime law. There has been an extraordinary development in this area of the law, of which *The Hate Debate* itself is evidence. Among the reasons that this development is particularly striking is that it has taken place over so short a period of time. Typically, when one does comparative work and discovers a dramatic change, there are two possible explanations: first, something has truly changed, the topic under study is a dynamic one, caught at a liminal time; or, second, the issue was not understood well enough the first time round. It is my hope that the former is the correct explanation here, although I cannot deny that I still fear the latter may be the case.

In this essay I set out a framework for understanding bias crimes, using the American context as a point of departure. I then sketch the background of British bias crime law, along with the case for understanding recent developments as indeed an instance of dramatic legal change. Finally, I offer some tentative observations as to the reasons for these changes, or at least some of the reasons for these changes, and the implications of these observations for using bias crime law as a window into society's understanding of itself as a multicultural entity. Whereas today the Runnymede Trust report on *The Future of Multi-Ethnic Britain* calls for a nation that sees itself as a 'community of communities' (Commission for the Future of Multi-Ethnic Britain 2000), it is not so very long ago that George Santayana dryly observed that the Englishman 'is relieved if only natives will remain natives, strangers, and at a comfortable distance from himself' (Santayana 1922).

The nature of bias crimes[2]

Bias crimes are the criminal manifestation of prejudice. They may be distinguished from parallel crimes—crimes that are similar in all manner but for the absence of bias-motivation—in terms of the mental state of the actor as well as the nature of the harm caused. A parallel crime may be motivated by any one of a number of factors, whereas bias crimes are motivated by a specific, personal and group-based reason: the victim's real or perceived membership in a particular group. Different bias

37

crime laws cover different groups. In the United States every bias crime law covers race and ethnicity in some form. Many also include religion, some sexual orientation, gender or other characteristics.

Bias crimes thus assault victims not only physically but at the very core of their identity, causing a heightened sense of vulnerability beyond that normally found in crime victims. Perhaps the most dramatic outcome affects victims of bias crimes directed at racial minorities whose experience of the attack provokes a sense of racial stigmatization and its resulting harms (cf. Allport 1954:148–9, Goffman 1963:7–17, 130–5, Page 1984). The stigmatized individual may experience clinical symptoms (cf. Clark 1965:82–90) and social symptoms (cf. Katz 1981, Kiev 1973:416, 420–4, Kitano 1974:125–6). Bias-motivated violence carries with it the clear message that the target and his or her group are of marginal value.[3] Stigmatization of bias crime victims is not limited to racially motivated bias crimes or to minority group victims. Group-motivated crimes generally cause heightened psychological harm to victims over and above that caused by parallel crimes.

The impact of bias crimes reaches beyond the harm done to the immediate victim or victims of the criminal behaviour. There is a more widespread impact on the 'target community' that shares the group characteristic of the victim, and an even broader based harm to the general society. Members of the target community do more than sympathize or even empathize with the immediate bias crime victim.[4] Members of the target community of a bias crime perceive that crime as if it were a direct attack on themselves. A cross-burning or a swastika-scrawling directed against an individual will not just call up similar feelings on the part of other Blacks or Jews. Rather, members of these target communities may experience reactions as if they had experienced an actual threat or attack from this very event (cf. Elias 1986:116, Karmen 1990:262–3, Levin and McDevitt 1993:220–1, 234).

Finally, the impact of bias crimes may spread well beyond the immediate victims and the target community to the general society. Such crimes violate not only society's general concern for the security of its members and their property, but also the shared values of equality among its citizens, and racial and religious harmony in a multicultural society.

This societal harm is, of course, highly contextual. We could imagine a society in which racial motivation for a crime would concern no other societal values than those violated by a criminal act motivated solely by the perpetrator's dislike of the victim's eye colour. This notion of contextuality in turn helps us understand which categories should and should not be included in a bias crime law. The characteristics that ought to be included are those that concern societal fault lines, divisions that run deep in the social history of a culture. In the United States, the strongest case is for race. Racial discrimination, the greatest American dilemma, has its roots in slavery, the greatest American tragedy. Strong cases can also be made for the other classic bias crime categories: colour, ethnicity, religion and national origin. The very act of determining which groups will be included in a bias crime law is a legislative and thus social determination of social fault lines.

Bias crimes in Great Britain

Bias-motivated violence is a problem of long standing in Great Britain. Only relatively recently, however, has British law formally recognized this problem.

Violence directed against the 'other' in Britain may be traced back to the early stages of the millennium. After the coronation of Richard I in 1189, Jews were massacred in London and in York. Indeed, in 1290, Jews were expelled from England altogether (Nicolson 1974). People of colour—from Africa, Asia and the Middle East—have lived in Britain, primarily in England, since at least the sixteenth century. Their experience too was one of separation from the main community, violence and, in 1596, attempts at mass deportation (cf. Banton 1959, Fryer 1984, Fryer 1988).

It was only in the twentieth century that large numbers of members of ethnic minorities began to live in Great Britain. During the First World War and the decades that followed, and particularly in the years immediately following the Second World War, people from colonies or former colonies came to Britain. The earlier part of this period saw both times of racial violence—such as the race riots in Liverpool, Cardiff and Glasgow in 1919—and times of almost complete segregation due to what was known as the 'colour bar'.

Total segregation became harder to maintain as the numbers of Blacks coming to Britain increased following the Second World War. Racial violence was a persistent problem, as evidenced by a series of racist riots in London and other urban areas where minority populations had begun to settle. The most notorious of these riots occurred in 1958, in Nottingham, and in the West London neighbourhoods of Notting Hill, Kensal New Town, Paddington and Maida Vale. In the years that followed, racist violence continued throughout Britain but did not occupy a position of any prominence on the political landscape (Bowling 1998:29–57).

The British legal system did not begin to address the problem of racial violence until the mid-1960s, and even then there was no recognition of bias crime as a particular social phenomenon. Rather, the focus of legislative efforts was on incitement to racial violence. The violence itself, it was presumed, could be addressed by existing general criminal legislation.

The first substantive criminal civil rights sanctions under British law are found in the prohibition of incitement to racial hatred in the Race Relations Act 1965.[5] This provision made it a crime to publish or distribute written matter or to use words in a public place or at a public meeting that are 'threatening, abusive or insulting' if done 'with intent to stir up hatred against any section of the public in Great Britain distinguished by colour, race, ethnic or national origins'.[6] In addition to specifically requiring this 'intent', the law also required the element of an objective result: that the words or matter actually be likely to 'stir up hatred against that section on grounds of colour, race, ethnic or national origins'.[7]

The racial incitement law was revised and now forms part of the Public Order Act 1986.[8] 'Racial hatred' is defined as 'hatred against a group of persons in Great Britain defined by reference to colour, race, nationality (including citizenship) or ethnic or national origins'.[9] The Public Order Act 1986 proscribes the use of words—oral or written—or behaviour that is 'threatening, abusive, or insulting' and is either intended 'to stir up racial hatred, or having regard to all the circumstances racial hatred is likely to be stirred up thereby'.[10] The act also criminalizes possession of racially inflammatory material with intent to display, publish, distribute or broadcast, if that actor either intends to stir up racial hatred, or under the circumstances, is likely to do so.[11]

The proscriptive language of the racial hatred law appears to permit either a subjective—intends to stir up racial hatred—or objective—racial hatred is likely to be stirred up—standard for guilt. The apparent negligence standard, however, is largely if not completely eliminated by the defences provided by the law. It is a defence, for example, that an actor who did not intend to stir up racial hatred 'was not aware that [his or her words or behaviour] might be threatening, abusive or insulting'.[12] So understood, the crime of incitement to racial hatred requires either purpose or knowledge, or at minimum a kind of recklessness with respect to causing the harms associated with racial hatred.[13]

Two issues bear special mention with respect to the crime of racial incitement. First, even with the relative easing of the

Crown's burden under the Public Order Act 1986, there has been a reluctance on the part of prosecuting authorities in Britain to bring cases for incitement to racial hatred. Attorney Generals have avoided bringing cases with a strong probability of losing for fear that unsuccessful cases of racial incitement may damage race relations rather than help them (Rozenberg 1987:138–9).[14] Law enforcement officials have also expressed a more concrete source of frustration in enforcing this law: distributors of hateful pamphlets and flyers, even in a pre-e-mail world, are virtually impossible to identify.[15]

Second, the provisions of the 1986 law, as was true of its 1976 and 1965 predecessors, do not reach bias crimes *per se* but rather incitement to racial violence. Perhaps the closest thing to a bias crime law that existed in Great Britain prior to 1998 was to be found in the Football (Offences) Act 1991.[16] This statute proscribes such behaviour as throwing objects towards the players or spectators and going on to the playing field. In addition to these more prosaic aspects of regulating conduct during football matches, the law criminalizes 'chanting of an indecent or racialist nature'.[17] 'Racialist' chanting is defined as 'threatening, abusive or insulting to a person by reason of his colour, race, nationality (including citizenship) or ethnic or national origins'.[18]

The Joint Committee against Racialism's 1981 report to the Home Secretary on racial violence may, in fact, mark the starting point of British bias crime law (Joint Committee 1981). Thereafter, the Home Secretary ordered the first official study of racially motivated violence, which was followed by various efforts to measure and to address the problem, leading, by the mid-1990s, to a much heightened awareness of the issue (cf. House of Commons 1994, Bowling 1993, Bowling 1998). Continued study by the Home Office demonstrated disturbing evidence of the persistence of the problem, but also encouraging evidence of increased understanding of its causes and dimensions (cf. Sibbet 1997).

Nonetheless, other than the incitement laws, there was no specific crime of racially motivated violence. This omission was not due to oversight. As late as 1994, a private members' bill was introduced in Parliament. The Racial Hatred and Violence Bill would have expanded the reach of the Public Order Act 1986 to include racial violence itself.[19] The bill failed for lack of government support. The government at the time preferred to treat bias crimes generally, using existing laws that draw on the provisions of the Public Order Act 1986 that proscribe verbal assaults.[20]

The Labour government that came to power in 1997 raised the issue of racial violence in its programme and manifesto. This culminated in the Crime and Disorder Act 1998 provisions concerning racially aggravated crimes, the United Kingdom's first bias crime law.

The 1998 act created a 'penalty enhancement statute' (Lawrence 1999:92–4), which increases the severity of a penal sanction for crimes that are 'racially aggravated'. Certain enumerated crimes, when racially aggravated, receive enhanced terms of punishment under the law. For all other crimes, racial aggravation must be taken into account by the sentencing judge as a factor that increases the seriousness of the offence.[21]

The broader framework

Early scholarly reaction to the racial violence provisions of the Crime and Disorder Act 1998 ranged from mixed to critical.[22] It is not the purpose of this paper to evaluate the enforcement of this provision. I can, however, begin to offer preliminary observations about what this change in the law signals about British society.

The change in the law has occurred at an extraordinary time in Great Britain. On 22 February 1999, the so-called Macpherson Report—the findings and recommendations of the commission looking into the police investigation of the murder of Stephen Lawrence—was issued. Lawrence, a black teenager, was murdered in 1993, purportedly by five white youths. No one was ever convicted of the crime. The Macpherson Report highlighted 'institutionalized racism' in the British law enforcement system (Macpherson 1999, Cathcart 1999). Moreover, Britain is at a 'turning point' in its perception of itself as a multicultural society.[23] Issues of race and ethnicity have become part of the public dialogue in Great Britain as never before (Marr 2000, Phillips and Phillips 1998).

Not surprisingly, this heightened profile of the multi-ethnic nature of the British polity has been reflected in the criminal law. As theorists such as Emile Durkheim and, more recently, Joel Feinberg have articulated, punishment represents societal condemnation of certain behaviour, and thus a statement of societal values (Durkheim 1984, Feinberg 1970, Reiner 1984). Social cohesion thus emerges from the act of punishment. Through its choices of punishments, a society reveals in part the content of its values.

Criminal punishment, unique among official sanctions imposed by an authority, carries with it social disapproval, resentment and indignation. As summarized by the Royal Commission on Capital Punishment: 'the ultimate justification for any punishment is not that it is a deterrent, but that it is the emphatic denunciation by the community of a crime'.[24]

What happens when a legislature enacts a bias crime measure and it is signed into law? This act of lawmaking constitutes a societal condemnation of racism, religious intolerance and other forms of bigotry that are covered by that law and, of perhaps greater significance here, a formal awareness of the role of these groups in society. What happens if bias crimes are not expressly punished in a criminal justice system or, if expressly punished, not punished more harshly than parallel crimes? Here, too, there is a message expressed by the legislation. The message is that racial harmony and equality are not among the highest values held by the community. Perhaps, more accurately, the message suggests a lack of formal awareness of the status and role of ethnic, racial or other groups in the society. Simply put, it is impossible for the punishment choices made by the society *not* to express societal values.

The racial violence provisions of the 1998 Crime and Disorder Art are a powerful reflection of the evolving awareness in Britain of the multi-ethnic dimension of the society. In a monochromatic society—in reality or as perceived by its legal system—we would expect a bias-motivated assault to be punished in an identical manner to a parallel assault; the group bias-motivation of the crime is rendered largely irrelevant in such a society and thus not part of that which is condemned. In a multi-ethnic society, however, we would expect bias-motivated crimes to receive some special treatment by the criminal law, to reflect the harm caused by the motivation underlying the crime.

The treatment of bias crimes under British law thus offers a significant window into the evolving self-perception of British society with respect to ethnicity and multiculturalism. The role of groups in Great Britain today is at a critical stage of evolution. The Parekh Report speaks of Britain at a 'crossroads', faced with the 'recognition that England, Scotland, and Wales are multi-ethnic, multi-faith, multicultural, multi-community societies' (Commission for the Future of Multi-Ethnic Britain 2000). In such a nation, violence motivated by group bias will continue to receive special attention from both the law enforcement community, and the various communities that together comprise the society.

Notes

1   The title of this paper alludes to Bill Bryson's *Notes from a Small Island* (1996). Earlier versions were presented at

the Gilbane Symposium at Brown University, Providence, at the Institute for Jewish Policy Research, London, and at a lecture delivered at Lincoln's Inn, London. I am most grateful for the comments received on those occasions. This project has been supported in part by a grant from the Ford Foundation and in part by a research leave provided by Boston University.

2   For a more detailed discussion of the nature of bias crimes, their cause and their resulting harms, see Lawrence 1999:29–44.

3   Gordon Allport discusses the degrees of prejudicial action, from 'antilocution' to discrimination to violence (Allport 1954:56–9).

4   See, e.g., Minow 1990:221, stating the importance of empathy in combating discrimination in the United States.

5   Race Relations Act 1965 (1965 ch. 73, §6).

6   Ibid., §6(1).

7   Ibid.

8   Public Order Act 1986 (1986 ch. 64, §§17–29). The law on racial incitement had previously been revised as part of the Race Relations Act 1976 (1976 ch. 74, §70). The most significant change to the prior law concerned *mens rea*. Whereas the 1965 act required that the offending act be done 'with intent to stir up hatred' (1965 ch. 73, §6(1)), the 1976 act required only that, 'having regard to all the circumstances, hatred is likely to be stirred up against any racial group in Great Britain by the matter or words in question' (1976 ch. 74, §70(2)).

9 Public Order Act 1986 (1986 ch. 64, §17). This language tracks the language used in the Race Relations Act 1976 (1976 ch. 74, §§70(2), 70(6)).

10 1986 ch. 64, §18 (use of words or behaviour, or display of written material), §19 (publishing or distributing written material), §20 (public performance or play), §21 (distributing, showing or playing a recording), §22 (broadcasting).

11 Ibid., §23.

12 Ibid., §18(5).

13 Similar defences to those set out in section 18(5) and discussed in the text are found throughout the racial hatred provisions of the Public Order Act 1986: see 1986 ch. 64, §§19(2), 20(2), 21(3), 22(3–6), 23(3).

14 The approval of the Attorney General is required for charges to be brought under the racial incitement laws (1986 ch. 64, §27(1)). This requirement carries through a provision from the prior racial incitement laws: Race Relations Act 1976 (1976 ch. 74, §70(5)); Race Relations Act 1965 (1965 ch. 73, §6(3)).

15 This observation is based on the author's interviews with members of the Crown Prosecution Service charged with enforcing racial violence laws and members of the Metropolitan Police Service (Scotland Yard) Racial and Violent Crime Task Force.

16 Football (Offences) Act 1991 (1991 ch. 19).

17 Ibid., §3(1).

18 Ibid., §3(2).

19 See *Criminal Law Review*, 1994, 313–14.

20 See Public Order Act 1986 (1986 ch. 64, §4(1)).

21 Crime and Disorder Act 1998 (1998 ch. 37, §§82, 96).

22 See, e.g., Maleiha Malik's opinion that provisions of the 1998 law represent an important but not sufficient response to racial violence (Malik 1999:409); Fernne Brennan's that criminal law does not play a significant role in responding to racist behaviour in racial violence (Brennan 1999:17).

23 See, generally, the Parekh Report (Commission for the Future of Multi-Ethnic Britain 2000), and particularly chapter 1. I address the subject of Britain's evolving understanding of itself as a multicultural society in greater depth in a paper tentatively entitled 'Treatment of bias-motivated crimes in the United States and the United Kingdom'.

24 Royal Commission on Capital Punishment, Minutes of Evidence, Ninth Day, December 1, 1949, Memorandum submitted by the Rt Hon. Lord Justice Denning (1950).

References

Allport, G. (1954), *The Nature of Prejudice*, Cambridge, MA: Addison-Wesley.

Banton, M. (1959), *White and Coloured: The Behavior of British People towards Coloured Immigrants*, New Brunswick, NJ: Rutgers University Press.

Bowling, B. (1993), 'Racial harassment and the process of victimization', *British Journal of Criminology*, vol. 33, no. 2, 231–49.

———— (1998), *Violent Racism: Victimisation, Policing and Social Context*, Oxford: Clarendon Press.

Brennan, F. (1999), 'Racially motivated crime: the response of the criminal justice system', *Criminal Law Review*, 17–28.

Cathcart, B. (1999), *The Case of Stephen Lawrence*, London: Viking.

Clark, K. (1965), *Dark Ghetto: Dilemmas of Social Power*, London: Victor Gollancz.

Commission for the Future of Multi-Ethnic Britain (2000), *The Future of Multi-Ethnic Britain. The Parekh Report*, London: Profile.

Durkheim, E. (1984), *The Division of Labor in Society*, trans. W. D. Hall, Basingstoke: Macmillan.

Elias, R. (1986), *The Politics of Victimization*, New York: Oxford University Press.

Feinberg, J. (1970), 'The expressive function in punishment', in Joel Feinberg, *Doing and Deserving*, Princeton, NJ: Princeton University Press.

Fryer, P. (1984), *Staying Power: The History of Black People in Britain*, London: Pluto Press.

———— (1988), *Black People in the British Empire*, London: Pluto Press.

Goffman, E. (1963), *Stigma: Notes on the Management of Spoiled Identity*, Englewood Cliffs, NJ: Prentice-Hall.

House of Commons (1994), *Racial Attacks and Harassment*, Home Affairs Committee, Third Report, vol. 1, London: HMSO.

Joint Committee against Racialism (1981), *Racial Violence in Britain 1980*, London: Joint Committee against Racialism.

Karmen, A. (1990), *Crime Victims: An Introduction to Victimology*, 2nd edn, Pacific Grove, CA: Brooks/Cole Publishing.

Katz, I. (1981), *Stigma: A Social Psychological Analysis*, Mahwah, NJ: Lawrence Erlbaum.

Kiev, A. (1973), 'Psychiatric disorders in minority groups', in P. Watson (ed.), *Psychology and Race*, Chicago: Aldine.

Kitano, H. H. L. (1974), *Race Relations*, Englewood Cliffs, NJ: Prentice-Hall.

Lawrence, F. (1999), *Punishing Hate: Bias Crimes under American Law*, Cambridge, MA: Harvard University Press.

Levin, J. and J. McDevitt (1993), *Hate Crimes: The Rising Tide of Bigotry and Bloodshed*, Boulder, CO: Westview Press.

Macpherson, W. (1999), *The Stephen Lawrence Inquiry: Report of an Inquiry by Sir William Macpherson of Cluny*, London: The Stationery Office.

Malik, M. (1999), '"Racist crime": racially aggravated offences in the Crime and Disorder Act 1998 Part II', *Modern Law Review*, vol. 62, 409–24.

Marr, A. (2000), *The Day Britain Died*, London: Profile.

Minow, M. (1990), *Making All the Difference: Inclusion, Exclusion, and American Law*, Ithaca, NY: Cornell University Press.

Nicolson, Colin (1974), *Strangers to England: Immigration to England 1100–1952*, London: Wayland.

Page, R. M. (1984), *Stigma*, London and Boston: Routledge and Kegan Paul.

Phillips, M. and T. Phillips (1998), *Windrush: The Irresistible Rise of Multiracial Britain*, London: HarperCollins.

Reiner, R. (1984), 'Crime, law and deviance: the Durkheim legacy', in Steve Fenton (ed.), *Durkheim and Modern Sociology*, Cambridge: Cambridge University Press.

Rozenberg, J. (1987), *The Case for the Crown: The Inside Story of the Director of Public Prosecutions*, Wellingborough: Equation.

Santayana, G. (1922), *Soliloquies in England, and Later Soliloquies*, London: Constable.

Sibbitt, R. (1997), *The Perpetrators of Racial Harassment and Racial Violence*, Home Office Research Study 176, London: Home Office.

4

SOME PEOPLE ARE MORE EQUAL THAN OTHERS

Peter Tatchell

In George Orwell's *Animal Farm*, all the animals were equal but some were more equal than others. The pigs received special privileges denied to other farmyard creatures. More than half a century after Orwell wrote his dystopian satire, the British government proclaims equality for all, but legislates greater equality for a few. We see this two-tiered system of citizenship and civil rights in the laws prohibiting discrimination in Britain: only discrimination based on race, sex and disability is illegal. This leaves other forms of discrimination lawful by default, including discrimination on the grounds of age, religion, sexual orientation, political opinion, HIV status, language and genetic inheritance.

Under the laws on blasphemy and incitement to hatred, there are also special rights for certain communities but not others. Even in cases of serious violent crime, not everyone is entitled to equal protection. Many crimes involving violence, or threats of violence, are motivated by prejudice and hostility towards the victim because of their racial, sexual or religious background. The perpetrators of these hate crimes go out of their way deliberately to target members of minority communities they despise. As well as victimizing Jewish, black, Asian and gay people, they also often vent their hatred on Travellers, communists, transsexuals, refugees and people with HIV. Instead of cracking down on all prejudice-inspired attacks, the official British government policy on hate crimes seems to be that some victims should be granted privileged legal protection and that all other victims should be ignored.

It was not always like this. When he was in opposition as Labour's Shadow Home Secretary, Jack Straw recognized the many different manifestations of hate crimes: violence, threats, abuse, intimidation and harassment. He also acknowledged the diverse communities affected, and the need for comprehensive legislation to protect all vulnerable peoples. Indeed, on 19 February 1997, just a few months before the general election that brought Labour to power, Straw addressed a lesbian and gay human rights meeting in the Grand Committee Room at the House of Commons. He quoted from the Stonewall group's national survey of homophobic hate crimes, *Queer Bashing* (1996), which found that a quarter of lesbians and a third of gay men had been violently attacked because of their homosexuality. One in three had suffered homophobic harassment, including threats, blackmail, vandalism, hate letters and graffiti. Three-quarters had been subjected to anti-gay verbal abuse. Arguing that 'the violence and fear to which gay people are subject is something which diminishes us all', Straw concluded by endorsing 'the need for more effective action to prevent and detect crimes in which there is a homophobic motive'.

After Labour's election in 1997, however, nothing more was heard about this concern for the victims of queer-bashing violence. Homophobic hate crimes were eased off the government's agenda, together with Labour's other pre-election promises to the lesbian and gay community. Instead of honouring its pledge to end the ban on gays in the military, the new government fought in the European Court of Human Rights (ECHR) to maintain the exclusion of homosexual personnel from the armed forces. It only relented when the ECHR compelled it to do so. The promised equalization of the age of consent was quietly shelved until the ECHR ruled that the discriminatory gay age of consent of 18 was illegal, which required the government eventually to equalize the consent laws three years later.

The unwillingness of the government to pursue its pre-election pledge to crack down on homophobic hate crime was particularly odd. Even people who are normally unsympathetic towards homosexual issues tend to regard assaults on lesbians and gay men as unacceptable. Action against anti-gay attacks would have provoked little hostility and probably garnered considerable public sympathy—especially if it was part of a comprehensive measure to tackle all attacks motivated by bigotry.

Timid and conservative as ever, the Labour government preferred to appease homophobic Middle England rather than take a stand against queer-bashing violence. Ministers assumed, probably mistakenly, that ex-Tory voters who switched to Labour in 1997 would be alienated by action against homophobic hate crimes. The suffering of queers therefore had to be subordinated to Labour's election strategy for a second term.

Nothing changed until a chance encounter in December 1997. The government had just announced that its forthcoming Crime and Disorder Bill (CDB) would create a new offence of 'racially aggravated' crime. Hostility towards a crime victim because of their race would be treated as an 'aggravating factor' in incidents of violence, harassment and public disorder. The courts would be required to treat racial aggravation as increasing the seriousness of the offence and therefore to pass tougher sentences on the perpetrators.

The then Home Office Minister, Mike O'Brien, was invited to outline the government's CDB proposals on the BBC's late night current affairs programme *Newsnight*. As someone with expert knowledge of hate crimes against a minority community, I was invited to join the panel, together with Barbara Cohen of the Commission for Racial Equality (CRE). Welcoming the new legislation, Cohen highlighted the huge number of racist attacks on the black and Asian communities and the inadequacy of the existing legal framework to deal with them. Although I understood and supported her argument, I felt some unease about the government's plan to create a special category of racial offences, and to punish an offence more severely because it had a racial motivation. Shouldn't all crimes of violence be treated the same? Why should one criminal be dealt with more harshly than another, when both have committed a similar offence? Is it ever legitimate to judge crimes based on motivations rather than consequences? Despite these concerns, on balance, I concurred with the CRE view that the CDB's new offence of racial aggravation was justified and necessary as a way of signalling society's abhorrence of race hate crimes and its determination to stamp them out.

Moreover, there is an ethical and legal justification for treating hate-motivated violence differently. It is not the same as other acts of violence. Hate attacks are often organized and systematic, targeting people and subjecting them to continuous attack over many weeks, months or even years. The consequences for the victims are uniquely harrowing. In this sense, hate crimes are qualitatively different from the usually random, opportunistic nature of non-hate crimes.

There is also a credible argument that, although crimes motivated by greed or jealousy are deplorable, there is something particularly repugnant about those motivated by prejudice and intolerance. Targeting people because of who and what they are—on the basis of personal characteristics such as race or sexuality—is quite distinct from other offences. Such crimes not only damage the victims, they also threaten social cohesion and solidarity by stirring division and animosity. To preserve harmonious community relations, it is therefore right that hate crimes should attract more severe penalties.

My main intervention in the *Newsnight* debate was, however, to question why race hate crimes were being singled out for special attention. Shouldn't the legislation be broadened, I asked, to encompass all hate crimes affecting all vulnerable communities? As well as covering attacks on

Jewish, black and Asian people, the tougher penalties should, I argued, apply to all hate-motivated assaults, including those against Travellers, religious minorities, people with HIV, lesbians and gay men, and individuals targeted because of their political beliefs or opinions. What I wanted was comprehensive, all-inclusive hate crimes legislation.

The case for including lesbians and gay men within hate crimes legislation is overwhelming. A series of major surveys over the last ten-plus years has revealed the massive scale of homophobic violence. Questionnaires distributed by the Gay London Policing Group (Galop) at lesbian and gay pride festivals, from the late 1980s to the early 1990s, consistently found that a third of lesbians and gay men had been violently assaulted by attackers who were motivated by anti-gay hate. Similar findings were reported by the Home Office-funded Safer Cities project in South-east London during the 1990s.

A more recent and comprehensive nation-wide survey was conducted in 1999 by the National Advisory Group on Policing the Lesbian and Gay Communities, which works with police services throughout the country. Published as *Breaking the Chain of Hate* (1999), it found that 65.9 per cent of lesbian, gay and bisexual people had been the victim of at least one (and often more) homophobic hate crime. Of the most recent homophobic incidents, 29.4 per cent were verbal abuse, 13.2 per cent were threats and intimidation, and 22.7 per cent were violent assaults.

The most up-to-date statistics come from the Lesbian and Gay Census 2001, conducted by ID Research. Its survey of over 10,000 lesbians, gays and bisexuals in all parts of the

United Kingdom found that in the last five years 25 per cent have been victims of serious homophobic crime, including physical assault, hate mail, rape or sexual assault, blackmail and arson. Sixty-five per cent of the victims did not report the crime to the police, mostly because they feared police harassment or had no confidence that the police would be sympathetic or understanding.

Around one in ten of the adult population is lesbian, gay or bisexual for significant periods of their lives. This figure is broadly confirmed by major research projects in the United States and Britain. These include Dr Alfred Kinsey's *Sexual Behavior in the Human Male* (1948), the British Marketing Research Bureau study for the Health Education Authority in Britain (1989), and the US National Health and Social Life Survey (1994). Of this 10 per cent of the population that is homosexual or bisexual, around a quarter have suffered serious homophobic hate crimes. This would suggest that approximately one million lesbians, gays and bisexuals in the United Kingdom have been queer-bashed, sexually assaulted or subjected to blackmail, arson or menacing mail threats. The huge volume of these homophobic hate crimes is at least as great as the level of comparable racist offences.

I presented Mike O'Brien with the evidence of widespread homophobic violence and harassment, and outlined to him the inadequacy of existing legislation. He seemed to accept that there was a credible case for including homophobic hate crimes within the CDB, and arranged for me to meet him at the Home Office. Prior to our meeting, it was agreed that I should draft an amendment to the CDB covering all forms of hate offences. My amendment to Section 68 of the CDB extended the tough new penalties for racist crimes to all crimes motivated by

prejudice or hostility to the victim of the offence based on the victim's actual or presumed religious affiliation or belief, sexual orientation, political or other opinion, disability, sex, medical condition, national or social origin, gender identity or physical appearance.

The aim was to offer protection to all vulnerable individuals and communities. Based on existing evidence of hate crimes, my amendment focused on nine forms of prejudice-motivated attacks:

- religion (vandalism of synagogues and mosques, harassment of Catholics in Scotland, threats against Sikh and Hindu temples)
- sexual orientation (queer-bashing of lesbians, gays and bi-sexuals)
- political opinion (targeting of liberals and left-wingers by the BNP and Combat 18)
- disability (attacks on people with physical and learning difficulties)
- sex (crimes motivated by a hatred of women)
- medical condition (violence against people with HIV)
- national or social origin (anti-Traveller, anti-refugee and anti-Irish offences)

- gender identity (abuse and intimidation of transgender people)
- physical appearance (bullying those who are overweight or disfigured)

As I pointed out to Mike O'Brien, and later wrote to the then Home Secretary, Jack Straw, my amendment was simple, no-cost, comprehensive, practical and effective. Home Office officials confirmed that it conformed to parliamentary rules, and was well drafted and workable. After three months of consultation and negotiation, I was hopeful.

On 11 March 1998, I had my long-awaited meeting with Mike O'Brien at the Home Office. It was not the friendly, intimate, open-minded discussion that I had expected. The Minister was accompanied by half a dozen advisers. Very quickly, it became apparent that they had already decided, in advance of the meeting, to reject my amendment. Their mood was defensive and Mike O'Brien and his team went to great lengths to justify why the amendment was 'unacceptable'. There was no interest whatsoever in discussing how it might be reformulated in a more acceptable form.

In contrast to his sympathy for comprehensive hate crimes laws when we had debated the issue on *Newsnight* three months earlier, Mike O'Brien was adamant: the CDB should focus exclusively on race hate crimes and my amendment could not be accepted because it would 'dilute' this focus on racism. The Minister's reasoning in rejecting my amendment was later spelled out to me in a letter dated 3 April 1998. It was written by Mike O'Brien's private secretary, Jon Payne, presumably with his boss's approval. The arguments in this letter reflect the views expressed by the Minister during his meeting with me, and in subsequent parliamentary debates.

According to Jon Payne's letter, the Home Office could not accept my amendment because:

> *Racist crime poses a particular threat to the development of a stable society. Too many of our citizens suffer daily fear they will be attacked or harassed because of their racial background. This is totally unacceptable and poses a serious threat to good relations between communities.*

My rejoinder was that too many of our citizens also suffer unacceptable victimization because of their religion, politics, HIV status and sexuality. This is also a threat to social stability and good community relations. Singling out one form of hate crime for privileged legal protection is divisive and discriminatory, and a sure-fire way to create social resentment and disharmony. Those excluded from the legislation will feel that others are getting special rights and that they are being treated as second-class citizens, making them vulnerable to manipulation by far-right extremists. Racism wouldn't be alleviated; it would be exacerbated.

The Home Office also stressed:

> *The new offences in the bill are designed to give a clear message that racial violence and prejudice is a*

particular social evil which cannot be tolerated. We should not confuse that message by adding others to the bill, even though we acknowledge that others may face difficulties too. Any addition to include, for example, homophobic violence would soften the message that we want to send. We have decided that we want to focus solely on racist cases. We need to highlight the issue of racism.

My counter-argument was that protecting other vulnerable communities does not diminish protection for racial minorities one iota. Action on hate violence against Muslims or queers does not imply any lesser concern about attacks on black and Asian people. As I later wrote to the Home Office Minister: 'All hate crimes are a serious menace. All vulnerable social groups deserve equal protection. All perpetrators of all crimes of prejudice should be punished with equal severity.'

In order to meet the government's concern not to dilute the focus on racially aggravated crimes in Sections 22 to 26 of the CDB, I deliberately proposed that my amendment should be to Section 68. This separation of race and non-race hate crimes was, in my view, a regrettable but acceptable compromise to meet the government's desire not to detract from the strong signal it wanted to send to the perpetrators of race hate offences. Precisely where in the bill the amendment was inserted was not really important. What was vital was that it was inserted somewhere in the CDB.

Mike O'Brien was unmoved by this attempt to meet him halfway. He then raised practical objections to my amendment, which were reiterated by Jon Payne in his subsequent letter: 'A broad-based anti-prejudice crime bill would be enormously difficult to interpret.' Why?, I asked. If the Home Office can find a way of interpreting and enforcing new legislation on racial crimes, why can't it do the same for other prejudice-motivated offences? Several European countries and US states already have workable, comprehensive hate crime laws. If they can do it, why can't the United Kingdom?

The Minister's response was irrational, illogical and down-right insensitive. What had motivated his sudden, implacable opposition? Who knows? Was it pressure from his boss Jack Straw? The then Home Secretary had earlier ditched his pre-election pledge of action against homophobic violence—an ominous omen. As political insiders well know, once Jack Straw makes up his mind, his ministers—mindful of their political and personal loyalties, and on the lookout for career advancement—tend to follow.

Undeterred by Mike O'Brien's brush-off, I remained determined to get a backbench MP to sponsor my amendment. It was circulated to several supportive Labour and Liberal Democrat members. The Lib Dems responded immediately. Encouraged by their enthusiasm, I met with MPs Richard Allan and Evan Harris. Both were sympathetic to my idea of comprehensive hate crime protection, but cautioned against covering all the many different forms of hate crimes in a single amendment. They feared the parliamentary debate would get bogged down in the technical minutiae of the nine different hate crime categories. MPs who objected to one or two of these categories might feel compelled to vote against the whole amendment. In Richard Allan's view, it would be better to narrow down the amendment to the two most serious and commonplace forms of hate attacks: those against religious and sexual minorities. I could see the practical argument: it is best to win something rather than nothing. Somewhat reluctantly, I agreed and redrafted the amendment accordingly.

Ironically, at the very moment that I was rewriting my amendment to crack down on hate crimes against gay people and people of faith, religious supporters in the House of Lords were lobbying to amend the Human Rights Bill to preserve the right of religious institutions to discriminate against homosexuals. Shortly afterwards, they fought tooth and nail to block the equalization of the age of consent, and two years later they fought with equal ruthlessness to maintain the discriminatory Section 28. Rising to the challenge, the queer human rights group OutRage! issued a news release taking the moral high ground:

We argue that all forms of prejudice are wrong, but religious leaders insist that denying equal treatment to gay people is right. Despite Christian, Muslim and Jewish opposition to homosexual human rights, OutRage! will continue to support equality for people of all faiths and sexualities.

In the light of the religious crusade against queer equality in the House of Lords, Richard Allan decided that including religion within the amendment, alongside sexuality, might be a red rag to the fundamentalists of all faiths. He feared it would attract their attention and provoke a campaign inspired by religious bodies that could scupper the entire amendment. In late May, the religious dimension was therefore dropped, leaving the amendment to focus solely on homophobic hate crimes. This was a mere shadow of my original comprehensive, all-inclusive intention. It was far from satisfactory and not a compromise I would have made myself had I been an MP and in a position personally to sponsor the amendment. Unable to do anything different, I deferred to the judgement of Richard Allan.

The amendment, known as New Clause 17, was in the names of the Lib Dem MPs Richard Allan and Sir Robert Smith. It was debated on 11 June 1998 in Standing Committee B on the Crime and Disorder Bill. The most surprising contribution to the committee's deliberations came from the openly gay MP, Stephen Twigg. While backing action on homophobic violence in principle, he obligingly echoed the reservations of Mike O'Brien and declined to support the amendment, claiming he was 'not convinced' that it was the 'most effective approach'. When later asked to come up with an alternative amendment, he failed to do so. To some observers, it looked like his status as a gay MP was being used—rather cynically and shamelessly—to undermine the amendment and to shore up support for the government's hard-line opposition.

Home Office Minister Mike O'Brien began by rejecting the amendment with the argument that it was unfair to give homophobic hate crimes preferential treatment over attacks on women, religionists and the disabled. Yet only two months earlier I had offered an amendment to protect these and other victims of hate crimes, and he had turned it down. He then continued: 'We must use the Bill to send a sharply focused message on racial violence and harassment ... We cannot afford to complicate it if it is to be understood by racist thugs.' In other words, Mike O'Brien was suggesting that one of the CDB's main purposes was, in fact, pedagogic. But does anyone really believe that racist thugs read parliamentary bills or listen to parliamentary debates? Do they give a damn about ministers' intentions? If the CDB covered all hate crimes, would this encourage hate-mongers to conclude that the government was not serious about tackling racist offences?

Mike O'Brien went on to suggest that it was no big deal for the CDB to ignore attacks on the lesbian and gay community: 'Not being included is not equivalent to exclusion.' Pardon? 'Seeking to address one issue does not suggest a failure to recognize others', he added. Even more bizarrely, the Minister then claimed that the victims of anti-gay attacks were already receiving privileged treatment: 'The penalties for homophobic attacks are the same as for attacks on anyone else but in practice the sentence is likely to be higher because of the aggravating feature of homophobia.'

Tell that to the loved ones of gay murder victims! Too often the killers literally get away with murder by claiming the defence of 'homosexual panic': that they suffer from an irrational, uncontrollable fear and loathing of 'faggots' that compels them to kill the 'dirty queers'. Far from getting tougher sentences, as the ill-informed Minister boasted, queer-bashers often get sentences that are considerably lighter than other murderers.

The debate in committee then took the oddest turn of all. Mike O'Brien argued that opposing the homophobic hate crime amendment was an issue of equality:

> *Admittedly the sentences for racist offences will be raised, but if New Clause 17 is rejected the maximum penalties for homophobic attacks will remain in equality with those for the vast majority of the population. Gays will not regret achieving such equality: their case has always been to demand equality rather than special treatment.*

Well, not quite. Supporters of New Clause 17 were never seeking 'special treatment' in the first place. All we wanted was homophobic violence to be treated the same as racist violence and punished with equal severity. The rejection of New Clause 17 would mean that homophobic hate crimes, in common with other non-racist hate crimes, would be subject to lesser sentences than racial ones. This is a form of discrimination. Contrary to the Minister's misguided belief, it was no consolation at all that the victims of queer-bashing attacks would be equally disadvantaged as other victims of non-racist hate attacks.

Facing the prospect of certain defeat in a Labour- and Tory-dominated committee, Richard Allan withdrew his amendment. But not before he received assurances from Mike O'Brien that the government was committed to further action to 'tackle homophobic attacks' and that an amendment on queer-bashing violence 'could well be considered at a later stage'.

Surprise, surprise! These assurances came to nothing. Moreover, the working of the Crime and Disorder Act 1998 has never been monitored to see whether extending its provisions to other forms of hate crime might be practical and useful. We were had!

5

HATEMONGERS, DABBLERS SYMPATHIZERS AND SPECTATORS: A TYPOLOGY OF OFFENDERS

Jack Levin

Americans were shocked at the brutality of the three white supremacists who, in June 1998, were charged with James Byrd's murder in Jasper, Texas. John King, Lawrence Brewer and Shawn Berry beat the black hitchhiker until he was unconscious, chained him to their pickup truck and then dragged him down the road on his back for almost three miles to his death. For the first two miles, not only was Byrd alive, but he was also conscious. Only when he was decapitated by a boulder at the side of the road was the victim's suffering ended and his life mercifully ended.

Organized hate

Investigators discovered a Ku Klux Klan manual among the possessions carried by one of the suspects; and two of the suspects wore white supremacist body tattoos depicting the Confederate Knights of America. King, Brewer and Berry were definitely ardent admirers of the Klan, who used white supremacist propaganda and enjoyed being identified with white supremacist symbols of power.

In addition to the murder of James Byrd, there have been several high-profile hate crimes in the United States committed by the members of white supremacist organizations during the last few years (Fox and Levin 2001). In July 1999, twenty-one-year-old Benjamin Smith, a student at Indiana University, murdered a Korean graduate student and a black basketball coach at Northwestern University. He also fired bullets at a group of orthodox Jews, injuring six of them. Smith's mentor was twenty-seven-year-old Matthew Hale, head of the white supremacist group World Church of the Creator, who preached Ra-Ho-Wa: the inevitability of a racial holy war from which Whites would ultimately emerge the winners. He despised Jews, Blacks, Latinos and Asians, considering them to be sub-humans on the same level as animals. He also argued that Christianity was merely a tool of deception used by power-hungry Jews to nurture a mindset that would allow them to take over the world.

Then, a few weeks after Smith's rampage, Buford Furrow walked into a Jewish community centre in the Los Angeles area, where he opened fire on a group of children as they played. Furrow then shot to death a Filipino letter carrier who just happened to be in the wrong place at the wrong time. A photograph later released to the public showed Furrow a few years earlier dressed in a Nazi uniform at the compound of the racist organization known as Aryan Nations.

Just weeks after Furrow committed murder in Los Angeles, Larry Gene Ashbrooke went on a rampage with an AK-47 at Fort Worth's Wedgewood Baptist Church, where he killed seven people as they prayed. It turned out that Ashbrooke was a member of the Phineas Priesthood, an organized hate group whose members preach that Jews are the children of Satan. Why, then, had Ashbrooke targeted Baptists? The answer involves a proclamation by the Southern Baptist Conference urging its members to convert as many Jews as possible. For Ashbrooke, this would have been the ultimate blasphemy. If Jews are the offspring of the devil, then the last thing you would want is to convert them to your cause (Lamy 1996).

Organized hate groups provide the situational facilitators in whose presence hate violence becomes more likely to occur. Not unlike a gang or a cult, the organized hate group comes to represent the family of a newly recruited member. Typically, the members of organized hate groups have lacked a sense of belonging. They aren't getting along with their parents, can't make it at school with their peers and are forced to take dead-end jobs at best. But in Posse Comitatus, Aryan Nations, White Aryan Resistance, World Church of the Creator or the Klan, they gain what has been missing in their lives: a sense of belonging and a vague feeling of their own importance (Ezekiel 1995).

No more than 5 per cent of all hate crimes in the United States are committed by the members of organizations like the

Ku Klux Klan, Aryan Nations or White Aryan Resistance. Still, groups of white supremacists continue behind the scenes to inspire murder, assault and vandalism. They provide propaganda to individuals looking to justify their own hateful behaviour, train youngsters in the art of bashing minorities, recruit on college campuses and prisons and workplaces, and operate cable-access television programmes featuring interviews with one another. They encourage and support much larger numbers of violent offences committed by non-members who may be totally unsophisticated with respect to the ideology of hate: racist skinheads, alienated teenagers, hate-filled young men looking to have a good time at someone else's expense (Levin and McDevitt 1993).

The Internet and its thousands of hate websites provide hatemongers with a new-found degree of influence that extends well beyond their small numbers. Thanks to the Internet, for example, Mat Hale's World Church of the Creator has reached thousands of young people around the country who may have racist and antisemitic feelings, and are thrilled to learn that they are not alone in these beliefs.

Dabbling in hate

For hardened hatemongers, bigotry becomes the basis for a full-time preoccupation, if not a career. They join an organization that espouses racism or other forms of prejudice. They completely limit their friendships to those who agree with their bigoted beliefs. And they practise what they preach by waging a campaign of intimidation against the 'outsiders' they despise.

Yet, in everyday life, not all hate incidents are so clearly hate-filled. Certain individuals dabble in bigotry; they convert their prejudices into behaviour, but only on a part-time basis as a hobby, by going out on a Saturday night with their buddies, for example, to assault someone, to burn a cross or to spray-paint graffiti.

Dabblers are typically young people looking for a thrill—usually groups of teenaged boys or young adults—who aren't getting along at home, in school or on the job. They may hate themselves as much as they hate their victims. But in committing a hate crime, they gain what seems otherwise to be missing from their lives. They feel superior to the extent that they make their victim inferior. They are made to feel important by their actions in reducing their enemies to the status of garbage. Moreover, many hate attacks directed against Blacks, gays, Muslims, Latinos, Asians and Jews are committed by dabblers who gain 'bragging rights' with their friends at the same time that they fill the idle hours with excitement.

Dabblers typically do not limit their attacks to any particular group. The interesting thing theoretically is that a dabbler who hates people because they are black is also likely to hate people who are Latino or gay or Asian or Jewish or disabled (Sniderman and Piazza 1993). This lack of specialization in the selection of a victim probably reflects the dabbler's psychological need to feel good about himself at somebody else's expense. Our culture supplies the dabbler with a range of enemies whom it would be appropriate to vandalize, bash, threaten, intimidate or assault. He makes his selection from this range of cultural villains based on what is convenient at the time.

Being defensive

Not all dabblers are looking just for a thrill. According to research conducted by Jack McDevitt and myself (1995), a second type of dabbler is motivated to commit hate crimes that, from his point of view, are defensive. Such attacks are typically precipitated by a threatening episode: a gay rights parade, Blacks moving into a previously all-white neighbourhood, the first Latino or Asian student on a campus. Failing to elicit the desired response—such as the immediate withdrawal of the Latino family from the previously all-white neighbourhood—there may be an escalation of violence. A verbal attack by phone may become a personal visit with a firearm; vandalism may turn more deadly.

Those who argue that hate crimes have been increasing also note that inter-group competition has been on the rise (Olzak *et al.* 1996). Whether or not it is economically based, growing threats to the advantaged majority group since the early 1980s may have inspired a rising tide of hate incidents directed against members of challenging groups. Over the last fifteen or twenty years, there have been dramatic increases in inter-faith and inter-racial dating and marriage, migration especially from Latin America and Asia, newly integrated neighbourhoods, schools, college dormitories and workplaces, as well as gay men and lesbians coming out (and, in many cases, organizing on behalf of their shared interests).

Donald Green and his associates (1997) have shown that hate crimes occur most frequently in 'defended' white neighbourhoods, that is, predominantly white areas that have experienced an in-migration of minorities. Broadening Green's concept a bit, we suggest that dabblers in hate may defend any aspect of their lives they feel especially entitled to hold: not only their neighbourhood, but their campus, their dormitory, their office or their social relationships.

In a 1992 study of hate crimes reported to the Boston police, it was found that Asians and Latinos were the two groups at greatest risk of victimization. These are the 'new kids on the block', the newcomers who are seen as threatening the economic well-being of groups of Americans who have been in the country longer and who now feel they must protect their stake in it (Levin and McDevitt 1993, 1995).

According to the most recent census data, such 'defensive' hate attacks might be expected to increase over the next several years. In the 2000 Census, the number of Latinos soared, overtaking African Americans to become the largest minority group in the nation. More specifically, Latinos represented 6.4 per cent of the total population in 1980; today they make up 12.5 per cent (Rodriguez 2001). Similarly, the Asian population has grown by leaps and bounds, especially in and around large cities. In New Jersey, for example, there was a 94 per cent increase during the past decade. In Pennsylvania, the Asian population grew by 83 per cent (Armas 2001).

International conflict often generates the precipitating incident for the occurrence of defensive hate crimes. During the
1978 Iranian hostage crisis, numerous students from Iran were
harassed or intimidated on the streets of American cities. In the
midst of the Persian Gulf war, Iraqi students were assaulted on
college campuses around the country. Similarly, in the aftermath of the September 11th attack, anyone who spoke with a
foreign accent and appeared to have Middle Eastern origins
was at risk of victimization. During the three weeks following
the terrorist assault on the World Trade Center towers, there
were more than 300 reports of harassment and abuse filed with
the Council on American-Islamic Relations. In Mesa, Arizona,
a forty-nine-year-old Sikh Indian wearing a turban was shot
down in front of his petrol station. In Dallas, a Pakistani
Muslim was found shot to death in his convenience store. In
Huntington, New York, a Pakistani pedestrian was nearly run
down by a motorist who had threatened to kill her. In San
Gabriel, California, an Egyptian Christian was killed in his
grocery store.

Sympathizing with hate

Millions of Americans may not be active hatemongers or
even dabblers, but they agree in principle with those who
are. Such 'timid bigots' can be regarded as sympathizers:
their prejudiced attitudes exist generally at a verbal level
only (Merton 1957). They may repeat a joke to their like-

minded associates but that is as far as they are willing to go. Nonetheless, their voices give encouragement and comfort to those who express their hatred in discrimination or violence. Moreover, because of their refusal to co-operate with those who seek to bring bigots to justice, sympathizers also share responsibility for the acts that their sympathetic stance makes possible.

It would be comforting if we were able to characterize hate and prejudice as deviant, irrational or pathological behaviour, as an aspect of the domain of a few 'crazies' on the fringe of society whose psychoses are in urgent need of treatment by psychotherapy, psychotropic medications or both. Unfortunately, hate hardly depends for its existence on individual pathology or abnormal psychology. Nor is it a form of deviance from the point of view of mainstream society. Even if the admission of being prejudiced is unacceptable, hate itself is normal, rational and conventional. It is part of the culture—the way of life—of the society in which it exists, appealing typically to the most conventional and traditional of its members (Westie 1964, Barnett 1999).

Where it is cultural, sympathy for a particular hatred may become a widely shared and enduring element in the normal state of affairs of a group of people. Even more importantly, the prejudice may become systematically organized to reward individuals who are bigoted and cruel, and to punish those individuals who are caring and respectful of differences (Katz 1993). In such circumstances, tolerance for group differences may actually be regarded as rebellious behaviour, and those who openly express tolerance may be viewed as rebels.

Sympathizers draw their hate from the culture, developing it from an early age in relation to parents, friends, teachers and the mass media. As a cultural phenomenon, racism is as American as apple pie. It has been around for centuries and is learned by every generation in the same way that our most cherished cultural values have been acquired: around the dinner table, through books and television programmes, from teachers, friends and relatives (Levin and Levin 1982).

The cultural element of hate can be seen in its amazing ability to sweep across broad areas of a nation. Individuals separated by region, age, social class and ethnic background all tend to share roughly the same stereotyped images of various groups. In the United States, for example, some degree of anti-black, anti-Asian and anti-Latino racism can be found among substantial segments of Americans—males and females, young and old, rich and poor—from New York to California, from North Dakota to Texas.

At the cultural level, the emotional character of racial or religious hatred is reflected collectively in laws and norms that prohibit intimate contact between different groups of people. In the Deep South, Jim Crow laws created separate public facilities: 'Colored' and 'White' restrooms, waiting rooms, water fountains and sections on public buses. In the South African version of apartheid, Blacks were similarly restricted to living in segregated communities and could work among Whites only under the strictest supervision.

Spectatorship

The forces of spectatorship have existed in countries around the world, including the United States. In the agrarian South, for example, slavery was widely viewed as a necessary aspect of the southern economic order generally and the plantation system of agricultural production in particular. But the one in four white Southerners who owned slaves were not the only Southerners who benefitted from the enslavement of African Americans. Many more were spectators who never made money directly from slavery, but enjoyed being members of what was regarded as a superior caste and gained indirectly from the fact that Blacks were not allowed to compete with them for jobs.

Moreover, the willingness of so many Americans during the Second World War to play the role of spectator made possible the rounding up of thousands of Japanese Americans, even those who were American citizens, forcibly removing them from their homes, confiscating their property and relocating them to internment camps—army-style barracks ringed with barbed wire and military guards—located thousands of miles away, where many of them remained throughout the war (Kochiyama 2001).

Active cultural bigotry was only part of the story of sending Japanese Americans to internment camps. Knowing that they would be gone for some period of time, many of them sold their houses and personal property in a few days for next to nothing. Moreover, real estate agents eagerly bought up the land left by farmers of Japanese descent. Whites could have offered to rent the residences of their Japanese-American neighbours and associates, but very few made the effort. Even though many white Americans recognized the unfairness of forcibly relocating an entire group of fellow citizens, it was hard to discover anyone who had the courage—at the risk of being regarded as disloyal to the United States—of speaking out against government policy (Kochiyama 2001).

Spectators enjoy the advantages of bigotry, even if they believe in principles of democracy and equality of opportunity. Rather than participate actively, they just go along to get along, as bystanders to a situation that they may feel powerless to change. Of course, their very inactivity—the failure to act on their convictions—tends to give licence to those who are raving bigots. At the same time, spectators benefit from whatever advantages their group receives from the perpetuation of prejudice. As a result, they laugh along with their friends at the most bigoted jokes, they walk right by teenagers painting hateful graffiti and they make no effort to stop any scheme aimed at harassing black neighbours.

Hate begins in silence

In the United States, there are relatively few hate crimes reported to the police every year, and most of these are committed not by members of organized hate groups, but by dabblers in hate. In the typical hate offence, a group of bored and idle teenagers or young adults goes out on a Saturday night looking for someone to intimidate or assault. What often gets overlooked is that those who commit hate offences are encouraged and supported by two categories of citizens: first, by sympathizers with bigotry who would perhaps never commit a hate offence themselves but are only too thrilled that others do. Those in sympathy with hate draw their thinking from the mainstream culture in which hate is widely learned and shared by members of a society. The second set of individuals probably represent the majority of citizens. Whether or not they have internalized the cultural stereotypes and emotions, they nevertheless remain passive bystanders in the face of destructive bigotry. These are the citizens who benefit from the *status quo*.

Indeed, even those individuals totally lacking in personal hatred may be supportive of bigoted behaviour as a rational choice because they are convinced that a particular decision— even if distasteful in some of its aspects—will help either to bring them the wealth, prestige or power they believe that they richly deserve or to keep them out of harm's way. It typically takes more than a sympathetic attitude towards hate to create the conditions conducive for hate crimes to thrive and prosper. It also takes convincing a sufficient number of society's members that they will benefit from a decision in support of bigotry. In many cases, this means that they support the *status quo*, that they simply go along with the masses, that they become not activists but passive spectators.

Moreover, in cases where hate is being considered as a viable political option, ordinary citizens might take an active stance in favour of a particular law, leader, political party or public policy that supports or encourages hate. Under different circumstances, they might be respectful of differences; but under conditions in which hate and prejudice are rewarded, they easily become what Merton (1957) referred to as 'fairweather' liberals. Of course, such choices may not always perfectly reflect actual self-interest, only a perceived self-interest. The appeal of rational choice is complex, involving short-versus long-term interests, personal versus social identity, an array of objectives in the economic, psychological and social spheres, and differences in access to information about a law, leader, political party or policy (Brustein 1996).

Where sympathizers and spectators let the small incidents pass without response, hate can escalate into ever more serious offences. Interpreting silence as support and encouragement, hatemongers and dabblers are likely to take their tactics to a more dangerous level, stopping only when they have achieved their intended purpose.

In August 2001, for example, Donald Butler, a twenty-nine-year-old black resident of Pemberton Township, Pennsylvania, was targeted by two white supremacists who shouted racial slurs at him as he stood on the front lawn of his home. Perhaps seeing the verbal abuse against him as an isolated or trivial event, Butler's white neighbours did absolutely nothing to assure him of their support or indignation. Three weeks later, the same two hatemongers returned with baseball bats, this time invading Butler's home in the dead of night, when they brutally beat him and his wife. The Butlers escaped with stitches and broken bones, but they also felt hurt and alone, as if no one really cared. They have since relocated to another community where their neighbours are more supportive and their safety seems less in doubt.

When thinking of the consequences of hate, we are likely to imagine the horrible violence in Bosnia, Israel or Northern Ireland. Or, we might think about the thousands of innocent people who lost their lives in the September 11th attack on the World Trade Center in New York City. But we should also never forget where hate begins: in the silence of ordinary people.

References

Armas, Genaro C. (2001), 'Asian-American population surges', *Boston Globe*, 11 March, A2.

Barnett, Victoria J. (1999), *Bystanders: Conscience and Complicity during the Holocaust*, Westport, CT: Praeger.

Brustein, William (1996), *The Logic of Evil. The Social Origins of the Nazi Party, 1925–1933*, New Haven: Yale University Press.

Ezekiel, Raphael S. (1995), *The Racist Mind: Portraits of American Neo-Nazis and Klansmen*, New York: Viking Press.

Fox, James Alan and Jack Levin (2001), *The Will to Kill: Making Sense of Senseless Murder*, Boston: Allyn and Bacon.

Green, Donald P., Dara Z. Strolovitch and Janelle S. Wong (1997), 'Defended neighborhoods, integration, and hate crime', unpublished manuscript, 23 June, Institution for Social and Policy Studies, Yale University.

Katz, Fred E. (1993), *Ordinary People and Extraordinary Evil*, Albany: State University of New York Press.

Kochiyama, Yuri (2001), 'Then came the war', in Joan Ferrante and Prince Brown, Jr. (eds), *The Social Construction of Race and Ethnicity in the United States*, 2nd edn, Upper Saddle River, NJ: Prentice-Hall.

Lamy, Philip (1996), *Millennium Rage. Survivalists, White Supremacists, and the Doomsday Prophecy*, New York: Plenum Press.

Levin, Jack and William J. Levin (1982), *The Functions of Discrimination and Prejudice*, New York: Harper and Row.

Levin, Jack and Jack McDevitt (1993), *Hate Crimes: The Rising Tide of Bigotry and Bloodshed*, New York: Plenum.

——— (1995), 'The research needed to understand hate crime', *Chronicle of Higher Education*, 4 August, B12.

Merton, Robert K. (1957), *Social Theory and Social Structure*, New York: Free Press.

Olzak, Susan, Suzanne Shanahan and Elizabeth H. McEneaney (1996), 'Poverty, segregation, and race riots: 1960 to 1993', *American Sociological Review*, August, 590–613.

Rodriguez, Cindy (2001), 'Latinos surge in census count', *Boston Globe*, 8 March, 1.

Sniderman, Paul M. and Thomas Piazza (1993), *The Scar of Race*, Cambridge, MA: Harvard University Press.

Westie, Frank R. (1964), 'Race and ethnic relations', in R. E. L. Faris (ed.), *Handbook of Modern Sociology*, Skokie, IL: Rand McNally.

6

HATE CRIME, VIOLENCE AND CULTURES OF RACISM[1]

Larry Ray
and
David Smith

This article presents some conclusions from a research project on racist violence conducted in Greater Manchester in the United Kingdom between April 1998 and September 2000. During the course of the research, in February 1999, the publication of the Macpherson inquiry into the murder of Stephen Lawrence placed the concept and politics of racist hate crime at the centre of British politics. Furthermore, the bombings in Brixton, Brick Lane and Soho in 1999 provided a context in which hate crime came to loom large in the popular imagination. Although the United Kingdom does not have a corpus of hate crime legislation comparable to that in the United States, the idea that crimes motivated by hatred of the victim's race, gender or sexuality should be punished more severely than other crimes has entered the British criminal justice system. The main legislative basis for this is the 1998

Crime and Disorder Act, which defines the offence of 'racially aggravated' assault and harassment. Some police divisions have gone further. For example, the Metropolitan Racial and Violent Crimes Task Force was established in 1998 to ensure that 'racially motivated and violent crime is prevented and when it occurs it is recognized, investigated thoroughly to agreed quality standards and reviewed objectively to enable lessons to be learned'. The Task Force records and pursues three types of hate crime—racist, violent domestic and homophobic—for which monthly and annual statistics are published. New legislative and police initiatives such as this have begun to reconfigure the ways in which the criminal justice system deals with certain types of violence.

The notion of 'hate crime' tends to conjure up the image of a self-conscious, possibly politically motivated, and brutal 'hater' whose actions are premeditated and ruthlessly planned. Clearly, such crimes occur and such criminals exist. Many ethnic and religious minorities are subject to routine and repeated harassment, violence and intimidation. But the image of the self-conscious 'hater' might not always best describe those prosecuted for racist crimes. One of the findings of our research is that many offenders whose crime has been recorded as having a racist dimension go to considerable lengths to deny any such intent. Our overall conclusion is that we do not necessarily best understand hate crime by focusing on the intent or motives of the offender. We need rather to examine the cultures of racism and of violence within which racist offending takes place.

Background: violence and 'hate crimes'

The issue of hate crime and racist offending in particular has arisen in the past few years for a number of reasons. There has been extensive social movement activity, such as victim movements, anti-racism movements and lesbian–gay activism, directed towards changing the way we think about violence and its motivation. In more traditional thinking, violence threatened otherwise 'safe' places and came from the 'outside', often involving transitional spaces (deserted trains, subways, metro stations late at night) or psychologically disturbed individuals. But a major impact of gender and anti-racism politics has been to reconfigure understandings of violence and call into question the existence of 'safe' spaces. Violence or its threat arises within the home and the local community, and indeed from the dark places of our inner psyche. It is within, not outside; and nowhere is safe. The realization that many millions of people have participated in or condoned genocide during the twentieth century further contributes to the sense that hatreds and the possibility of violence are deeply rooted in society, not just in particular individuals.

Other social and cultural developments, however, have increased our sensitivity both to violence and to associated emotions of hatred. Modern societies are increasingly globalized and cosmopolitan so that social integration depends on our ability to recognize and negotiate cultural and ethnic difference. Both civil and criminal law, especially through concepts of human rights, have been important vehicles for establishing the principle of equality of treatment. Civil rights and equal opportunities legislation of the 1970s has now been supplemented with juridical protection against bias crime and victimization for reasons of membership of a particular social or cultural group. Underlying this has been a longer-term process of what one might call 'civilianization'. In times of mass warfare, reserves of hatred or at least antipathy towards foreigners were among the resources states could mobilize in the event of a military conflict. In a globalized, post-Cold War era in which it is less clear who are our enemies, hatred of foreigners becomes a potential public order problem, rather than a resource for state mobilization.[2] The acceptable expressions of national or more locally based hatreds are confined to symbolic confrontations, such as those provided by sport, especially football; and even in these settings there are clearly risks that the symbolic violence will spill over into the real thing.[3] This is part and parcel of an even longer-term change in public sensibilities regarding hatred and violence, one that the sociologist Norbert Elias described as the 'civilizing process' (Elias 1998:*passim*). The growth of increasingly mannered social interactions, roughly from the seventeenth and eighteenth centuries, has been accompanied by an increased public intolerance of violence. Repugnance towards physical violence has also become greater as the thresholds of shame and embarrassment surrounding the body have moved: acts once performed publicly, such as defecation and sexual intercourse, have become intensely private.

What follows from this? On the one hand, societies have manifestly not become less violent than in the past; crimes of violence in the United Kingdom rose steeply during the last quarter of the twentieth century. Yet the respect and recognition of human rights and juridical enforcement of the right to equality of treatment has been a major basis for social integration in recent decades. Along with this, public sensitivities towards violence and hatred have increased in that conduct that might once have been regarded as publicly acceptable is no longer so seen.[4] This creates a powerful context for initiatives against hate crimes that seek to punish not only the act, such as an assault, but the intention, underlying motive and reasons for selection of the victim. Yet how do these intentions relate to real offending behaviour and its causes?

Research on racist violence

We started with two basic ideas. First, that we should try to understand the motives of perpetrators of relatively serious racist attacks, rather than focusing on 'routine' acts of harassment and abuse, such as those described by Rae Sibbitt (1997). Second, that we should explore the connections between the motives of individual perpetrators of racist attacks and the racist sentiments in the communities from which they came.[5] We were also interested in the responses of the police, the probation service and other agencies to local problems of racist violence.

In the aftermath of the murder of Stephen Lawrence, there are two important public perceptions of racist violence: that racist crime is usually committed by strangers, and that the motives of offenders are transparent and often politically motivated. However, our research points to a different pattern. Offenders and victims are quite likely to know each other, though not well. Offenders frequently do not have an explicitly articulated racist motivation but are likely to show a high degree of ambivalence in describing their violent behaviour, often keen to neutralize its alleged racist dimension.

Urban restructuring and communities

Community, identity and racism should be understood alongside the broad fabric of patterns of social and economic development and their impact on peoples' lives. During the past two decades Manchester, like other British cities, has undergone a profound economic and social restructuring, with the decline of regional Fordist systems of production and consumption. Between 1972 and 1984, 207,000 manufacturing jobs were lost, three-quarters of them during the 1980s. During the same period the economic base of the city shifted towards the service and financial sectors, which account for 43 per cent of employment (Taylor *et al.* 1996). In the wake of these changes, many apparent certainties of the past have been undermined and the labour market has been divided into core, skilled insiders and largely unskilled outsiders. This has had an impact on communities once organized around industrial work and on the transmission of cultural expectations of masculinity and belonging.

In particular, for those excluded from new post-Fordist labour markets and cohesion strategies, resentment of difference and otherness can take the form of new violent exclusions and territorial defences. In these terms, borders become symbolic of transformations the city is undergoing. Symbolic boundaries of housing, access to transport and jobs are projected on to mental maps of the city, in which are inscribed ethnic notions of territory and belonging. Thus particular areas are designated as 'belonging' to particular ethnicities, a mapping that can be deployed to justify violent exclusion. Offenders in our survey usually lived in predominantly white, socially deprived and marginalized areas on the outskirts of the conurbation, and typically resented South Asians for their alleged economic success and the apparent solidarity of their family and community ties. Such tensions came to a head in Oldham and other north-west English towns in the summer of 2001. Notions of 'territory' and 'encroachment' were mobilized in the violent confrontations involving Asian and white youths, after several months of rising tensions and the increasing activity of fascist groups.

Patterns of offending

This socio-economic background structured the communities and life expectations of the localities in which many offenders in the study lived. The following are some of the main characteristics of these offenders.

- They were predominantly men: out of the 64 identified from probation records as possibly having a racist dimension to their offence, only 5 were women.

- Their average age was 24 years, with 48 being under 25. The method of sample selection (via the Probation Service) meant that our sample would exclude very young offenders; but, reflecting the probation caseload as a whole and indeed the overall demographics of known offenders, it was inevitable that the sample should consist of young men.
- 50 per cent were unemployed, although Manchester's core unemployment rate is 6 per cent. Those in employment tended to be in low-skilled and casual jobs with insecure futures.
- They tended to have a poor educational history: 64 per cent had no qualifications, consistent with the widely held view that young people who fail academically and occupy low-status positions exhibit the highest rates of violent offending.
- Over half referred to similar offences in the past, sometimes involving the same premises and individual victims, lending weight to the view that persistent harassment is common.
- However, they were non-specialists: 64 per cent reported convictions for other offences, mainly theft, assault and drugs. This suggests that racist offending is often part of a wider pattern of criminal behaviour.
- There was no clear pattern of articulated political motivation: they showed a low level of knowledge of racist organizations and little evidence of the assimilation of racist political ideology.

The respondents often displayed a lack of self-esteem, difficulty in articulating their identity and high levels of insecurity.

Some studies suggest that hate crimes are perpetrated by white youths against groups whom they consider inferior.[6] But our research suggests a more complex picture. Most respondents displayed a sense of shame (Scheff 1994) rather than an assertive superiority, and were ambivalent about their identity. They generally exhibited difficulties articulating any particular identity, and this uncertainty about their belonging and community was sometimes a source of frustration that reinforced hostility towards South Asian communities. The latter were constructed as having a culture and community that they, the subjects of our study, lacked.

Neutralization and denial

There are clearly instances of premeditated assaults and repeated harassment by committed racists. But in our study as in others, such as Sibbitt (1997), many offenders do not conform to the stereotype of white perpetrators who pick on random victims. The perpetrator often knew the victim, and incidents defined as 'racially motivated' often arose in the context of street confrontations and were often associated with alcohol consumption by the offenders. Moreover, offenders demonstrate repertoires of 'neutralization', that is, providing accounts of the offence that attempt to make it appear 'normal', thereby denying or mitigating its criminality. For example, one said: 'I didn't mean it [an offensive remark] and he knew that', and 'The police were trying to make it worse by calling it racist. The names were not that bad.' In this case racist abuse directed at a taxi driver was seen as a normal part of a dispute over the fare. In the context of another violent assault one respondent said: '... the eighteen-year-old lad comes out with a dirty big iron bar, and because I picked up a milk bottle and said "right you black bastard, if you want it, you can have it" that's a racist attack.'

The idea that racist language is not 'really offensive' and is part of a trade in insults in the course of a dispute was widespread. The perpetrators' families were often cited as not regarding the offending behaviour as racist or wrong. Offenders will often go to some lengths to try to show that the offence did not have any racist motivation. There are frequent claims that violence and verbal abuse were reciprocal in a situation of street confrontation in which offenders would often portray themselves as victims, not least of the alleged power and influence exercised by South Asian communities.[7]

However, these systematic neutralizations attest to (a) the social unacceptability of articulating racism, and also (b) the ambiguity of the notion of 'racist motivation'. In many cases racist abuse is deployed in a confrontation that had an ostensible origin unrelated to the ethnicity of the participants. However, in the very attempts to exculpate violence that they are deploying, they summon up a background culture of racism that regards such violence as legitimate. Thus in these racialized communities whiteness is a resource for offloading shame at being losers in the processes of socio-economic transformation. In this context we might be able to explain the specific intensity of racism against South Asians rather than

Blacks, who are often seen as sharing a macho street culture with young white men. Underlying this, we argue, is a sense of shame that is tied particularly to a crisis of masculinity and sense of lack: an inability to perform the culturally expected role of male 'hard grafter'. This in turn is manifested in a projection on to ethnic minorities of the attributes allegedly missing in their own lives: identity, social integration, belonging and economic success.

Cultures of racism

These considerations were supported by our study of perpetrators' communities. In one community in South Manchester, which was atypically homogeneously white, respondents in focus groups emphasized this difference and the separation of their community, as a white one, from the rest of Manchester. They identified themselves as a white integrated community, while nearby Rochdale was seen as 'rather alien, too many foreigners'. They exhibited nostalgia for working-class culture and the attributes of strength and masculinity. Languages of racism were infused with those of class resentment, for example, 'they rip you off', which 'they' were able to do by virtue of their economic success. This nostalgia for the lost world of industrial work was combined with an effeminized image of South Asians and with class resentment: 'At work they don't seem to do the same things: Not heavy work like on building sites, you don't see Pakis. They do corner shops, and businesses, money grabbers, not hard grafters. Blacks, they're more macho. More like us really.' Familiar urban myths circulate: 'they get a good deal, they get what they want ... they have special areas done up'. Complaints about overcharging in shops are commonplace as are arguments over credit but, again, racist stereotypes are being deployed in the course of economic and cultural conflicts. Fear and anxiety arising out of a limited identification with one group becomes aggression against another. Violence 'resolves' contradictions by making them disappear; they no longer need to be negotiated and the meanings of 'whiteness' remain undisclosed and ambivalent.

Individual offenders and the wider culture

Our research indicates that racism is complex and contradictory and is intertwined with cultural acceptance of violence as a way of resolving problematic situations. Interventions in this area will need to address both violence and racism as separate though related issues. While there are few hard-core racists, it is significant that wide and deep cultures of racism are deployed in confrontations that have ostensibly non-racial origins. Violence and racism intertwine and trigger one another in complex configurations of exclusion and scapegoating, which are sustained by myths of the power and influence exercised by the minority community. There are both cultural and economic dimensions to violent racism: the subjects in our study had few resources, little cultural capital, were excluded from smart housing, employment and life chances. Again, interventions would need to address these underlying conditions, or at least assist offenders to find ways of breaking out of low-paid, low-skilled forms of employment. This is especially so if, as we suggest, shame is externalized as violence directed at perceived symbols of cosmopolitan culture and economic success. Finally, although the current initiatives to address hate crimes have an important role in profiling and, we hope, deterring, this offending, this category of offence risks focusing on individual motives and intentions while overlooking the extent to which racist offending is embedded in local and wider cultures.

Notes

1   The findings reported in this paper are based on the ESRC research project, 'Racial violence in Greater Manchester', carried out by David Smith (Lancaster University), Larry Ray (University of Kent at Canterbury) and Liz Wastell (Greater Manchester Probation Service) (ref: L13325019). Further research is required to assess the extent to which they might be generalized across Britain.

2   This needs to be expressed cautiously in the wake of the September 11th atrocities and subsequent military actions, which could cause this view to be revised. However, it identifies a trend of *longue durée*, not towards a world without conflict but towards increasingly fluid and post-national forms of conflict in which specific enemies are difficult to define.

3   See, for example, Dunning *et al.* 1986.

4   Dunning *et al.* 1987, for example, argues that during the 1910s and 1920s in Britain violence at election times was regarded by the police as normal and not requiring intervention.

5   The importance of these connections is stressed by Hewitt 1996.

6   See, for example, Messerschmidt 1994.

7   There are clear similarities here between this kind of racist hostility towards Asians and typical forms of anti-semitism. In both cases the stigmatized group is constructed both as powerful and as possessing forms of belonging and community that are not available to 'ordinary' people.

References

Dunning, E. G., P. Murphy and J. Williams (1986), 'Spectator violence at football matches: towards a sociological explanation', *British Journal of Sociology*, vol. 37, no. 2, 221–44.

Dunning, E. G., P. Murphy, T. Newburn and I. Waddington (1987), 'Violent disorders in twentieth century Britain', in G. Gaskell and R. Benewick (eds), *The Crowd in Contemporary Britain*, London: Sage.

Elias, N. (1998), *The Norbert Elias Reader*, ed. J. Goudsblom and S. Mennell, Oxford: Blackwell.

Hewitt, R. (1996), *Routes of Racism*, Stoke-on-Trent: Trentham Books.

Messerschmidt, J. (1994), 'Schooling, masculinities and youth crime by white boys', in T. Newburn and E. Stanko (eds), *Just Boys Doing Business*, London: Routledge, 81–99.

Scheff, T. J. (1994), *Bloody Revenge: Emotions, Nationalism and War*, Boulder, CO: Westview Press.

Sibbitt, R. (1997), *The Perpetrators of Racial Harassment and Racial Violence*, Home Office Research Study 176, London: Home Office.

Taylor, I., K. Evans and P. Fraser (1996), *A Tale of Two Cities: Global Change, Local Feeling and Everyday Life in the North of England*, London: Routledge.

7

THE USES AND LIMITS OF PROSECUTING RACIALLY AGGRAVATED OFFENCES

Elizabeth Burney

The law creating specific 'racially aggravated' offences came into force in Britain in October 1998, as part of the new Crime and Disorder Act. Like much else in that act, it was the fulfilment of policies adopted by the Labour Party when still in opposition although, as we shall see, it goes considerably further than the original pledge to enact a law against 'racially motivated' crime. I will not rehearse all the arguments in favour of such a law, except to sum them up with the proposition that crimes against individuals based on their ethnicity potentially affect much wider circles of people with similar identities and can help to destabilize whole communities in which positive social interaction depends on racial tolerance (Iganski 2001, Lawrence 1999). Britain's gradual development as a multiracial nation is seen to require legal protection if it is not to regress.

The question then is: what sort of law, and how is it applied? However ideal a legal instrument may be, it will still depend on police, prosecutors and courts to use it effectively, and will require the trust of the public to supply complaints and evidence. If there are difficulties and ambiguities in the law itself, any reluctance or scepticism on the part of key players will compound these weaknesses.

The government clearly intends that the law should be used in any context in which evidence of racial animus can be linked to an offence.[1] As guidance to Crown prosecutors makes clear, racially aggravated offences must always be treated seriously and should very rarely be dropped on 'public interest' grounds. Nevertheless, the range of 'seriousness' involved is quite wide, and the social contexts highly varied. This raises questions about the appropriateness of the criminal court for resolving incidents in which both the underlying criminality and the expression of racism may be slight. Or indeed about whether, even in more fraught situations, there may not sometimes be more appropriate methods than prosecution for dealing with racist crime. The second part of this essay will take a broader look at the adversarial versus the reconciliatory approach to some of the typical cases that may be prosecuted as racist offences.

The Crime and Disorder Act creates a number of new 'racially aggravated' offences based on existing offences of violence, public order, harassment and criminal damage. If the aggravated element is proved, substantially enhanced sentences can be imposed. A separate section of the act restates the established principle that any offence, not only those on the list, should be sentenced more heavily if there is evidence of racial aggravation.

The definition in section 28 of the act is important:

28 (1) An offence is racially aggravated[2] for the
purposes of sections 29–32 below if
(a) at the time of committing the offence, or
immediately before or after doing so, the offender
demonstrates towards the victim of the offence
hostility based on the victim's membership (or
presumed membership) of a racial group; or
(b) the offence is motivated (wholly or partly) by
hostility towards members of a racial group based
on their membership of that group.

Thus, it is not necessary to prove motivation—American experience has been cited to show the difficulty of this (Morsch
1991)—but sufficient that 'hostility' based on ethnicity and so
on has been demonstrated in the immediate context of the
basic offence. In practice, this almost always means that a
word or words relating to the victim's ethnicity have been
coupled with abuse. For example, in the case *R* v. *White*
(2001) the Court of Appeal found that an African-Caribbean
passenger who called a bus conductor who had accused him
of attempted theft a 'stupid African bitch' was guilty of a
racially aggravated public order offence. Public order offences
are those most frequently charged under the act, in the context
of racial abuse. A high bench-mark was set in the case of
Miller (1999), in which the defendant, a fare-dodger, threatened the Asian railway conductor with a torrent of racist

insults. A sentence of eighteen months was confirmed, three times the maximum for the basic, non-aggravated, offence of section 4 of the Public Order Act 1986 ('threatening, abusive or insulting words or behaviour, with intent to cause [the victim] to believe that immediate unlawful violence will be used against him'). Subsequently, the Sentencing Advisory Panel has indicated that it considers this particular sentence excessive, but still recommends a 40–70 per cent sentence enhancement for cases with a high level of racial aggravation (Sentencing Advisory Panel 2000).

It is sometimes argued that the legislation was unnecessary because there was already a sentencing principle, spelled out in the case of *Ribbans* (1995), that a racist element in an offence should carry a heavier sentence. However, the degree to which the principle was observed is questionable. As responses to the draft statutory proposals indicated (Iganski 1999), many practitioners welcomed legislation that would set clear signposts alerting police, prosecutors and courts to the importance of identifying and dealing with racist crime.

Despite this, it is all too apparent that the form of the legislation is in itself likely to undermine its aims. Its two-tier structure—the aggravated offences derived from underlying substantive offences—facilitates offers of pleas to the non-aggravated version. People will plead guilty to ordinary offences that they would probably have contested, for fear of a heavier sentence for a racist crime and of being labelled a 'racist'. Prosecutors may not always be able to resist the opportunity to avoid a contest.

This is likely to result in some cases not receiving the level of sentence suggested by the facts. If a case is tried in which evidence would support a charge of one of the racially aggravated offences, yet only the basic version is being prosecuted, the court cannot consider the evidence of racism and the sentence cannot take any account of it. This is because of the rule that nobody can be punished for an offence more serious than that on the charge sheet. Judges' hands are tied in a way that did not exist before the two-tier legislation was introduced.

Published statistics suggest significant differences among police forces in identifying and pursuing racially aggravated offences (Home Office 2000). Variations in the recording of racist offences do not always reflect variations in ethnic minority populations, and sometimes bear little relation to the separately recorded 'racist incidents' (which need not, of course, be criminal). The relatively high number of incidents and offences recorded by the Metropolitan Police does, however, reflect proportionally the capital's large and diverse ethnic minority population. The Met has a dedicated 'hate crime' unit (covering racial, homophobic and domestic violence crimes) and pursues an active prosecution policy. This is seen as an advance on practices largely devoted to supporting victims rather than obtaining criminal evidence. Another strand of policing is that associated with problem-solving methods in the context of multi-agency approaches to local crime and anti-social behaviour. This approach does not necessarily privilege prosecution over other methods of dealing with racist perpetrators.

This introduces the second theme of this essay. It serves no purpose for racially aggravated charges to be brought to court and then abandoned, or for evidence of a blatantly racist nature to be suppressed for procedural reasons. But, it must now be asked, is the court always the right place for dealing with cases in which the racial hostility displayed is a very minor element, or in which words referring to ethnicity may not even be genuinely 'hostile' (as opposed to ignorant, descriptive, flippant and so on)? And even where racist hostility clearly exists, but there are also opportunities, say, in a neighbourhood setting, to challenge racist behaviour by a range of less formal methods, does the public interest always demand that prosecution should take place wherever the evidence can justify it?

The type of cases charged as racially aggravated range from serious premeditated assaults (which are rare) to one casual word uttered in public and, as the Sentencing Advisory Panel has said, sentencing should reflect the degree of seriousness. Some people argue that, however slight the charge and the sentence, prosecution symbolizes the importance of confronting manifestations of racism. But there are other ways of marking disapproval and possibly providing more satisfaction for the victim. An informal warning may be enough to bring the message home to perpetrators and make them desist. One-off drunken insults shouted in the street—the stuff of many racially aggravated public order charges—might, depending on circumstances, be dealt with by means of a caution, perhaps conditional upon a written apology. The

Crown Prosecution Service (CPS) should be able to order a caution with an apology in appropriate instances in which cases are discontinued on public interest grounds. If English prosecutors had the same wide-ranging powers as Scottish procurators fiscal, more individualized alternatives to prosecution could be applied.

The power of the apology in the aftermath of hurtful behaviour should not be underrated (Tevuchis 1991), and is already built into the restorative aspects of the youth justice system. Particularly for young people—and perpetrators are often very young—this can be an educative exercise. Their language will very often parrot that of their elders and, indeed, it is arguable that, hearing racist language from parents, a young adolescent may have no concept of its wrongfulness. Schools have a great responsibility to instil other values, and to deal swiftly with racist bullying. There is widespread agreement that education, in the broadest sense, has to be the way forward in reducing racism in the long term.

Some racist incidents are so gross and gratuitous that prosecution must be pursued. Likewise, possibly the worst of all, the continual, prolonged and repetitive racist taunts and assaults, by neighbours or inflicted on shopkeepers and fast-food providers who may be the only visible representatives of an ethnic minority in a neighbourhood, have to be dealt with firmly and not left to be repeated indefinitely. The appalling story of the sufferings of the owners of a corner shop in Lancaster emerged in the case *Hussain and Livingstone* v. *Lancaster City Council*. Mr Hussain claimed redress from the council for not imposing sanctions on those of its tenants who were said to be responsible. Councils who are social landlords do have considerable power, often thought to be more effective than prosecution, to impose injunctions and if necessary obtain eviction on grounds of racist behaviour.

When prosecuting such cases, evidence may have to be built up over time from a range of sources, and requiring the co-operation of police, local authorities and other agencies. This is harder, but arguably far more important, than obtaining easy convictions for one-off public order offences.

As published cases show, many crimes are racially aggravated by reason of a word or two in the course of a dispute over some other matter, with no evidence of racial motive. In the United States these so-called 'garden fence' cases are not covered by hate crime law. The law arguably comes down rather hard on people who throw in ethnic references along with insults arising from, say, a 'road rage' incident. On the other hand, prosecution serves to expose underlying racism and to draw a clear line on what is not acceptable. There may sometimes be a difficult choice—and the feelings of the victim may be decisive—between informal action, as mooted above, and a prosecution. The CPS might need to consider more often whether the public interest lies on one side or the other. In rare instances the zealous application of current guidelines threatens to bring the law into disrepute. (We do not, of course, hear much about cases dropped for the opposite reasons.) In a widely reported case in the spring of 2001 two boys aged ten and eleven, who had allegedly hit a classmate and called him a 'Paki bastard' in response to being teased by him for being fat, were prosecuted for racially aggravated common assault. (Eventually, the aggravated charges were dropped and the boys obtained absolute discharges.)

Defendants prosecuted for racially aggravated offences, even if they admit the words that constitute the charge, often protest vehemently against being branded as 'racists'. In contested cases, people are worried not only by the prospect of a heavier sentence, but by the shame of a 'racist' label. This suggests that the law is pushing at an open door. Attitudes are, of course, notoriously slippery: people who will happily refer disparagingly to 'Pakis' or 'Blacks' in normal discourse may still be indignant if accused of being racist. Publicly, at least, racism is seen as unacceptable. It could be a risky strategy to pursue too many of the less seriously aggravated cases for the sake of proving the importance of the law, because in so doing public acceptance of the principle behind it could wither.

A broader objection might be that individual prosecutions, by identifying defendants as 'racists', set them apart from the rest of us as though their actions or words had nothing to do with attitudes or mindsets that are widespread, even endemic. Serious race hate is fortunately rare—which is why the label 'hate crime' for these offences is so misleading—but probably most people harbour some kind of prejudice that, hopefully, they recognize and constrain. The people who get prosecuted for racially aggravated offences are often too ignorant or unsophisticated to exercise self-control. Typically, they are people already labelled as lower-class 'yobs' or troublemakers. They must certainly be restrained from the pain they inflict on victims, and in bad cases punished severely. But we should not forget that there are many other people, in positions of power and influence, who would never dream of committing offences, aggravated or otherwise, but whose effect on race relations has the potential for other, more insidious, harms.

A strategy that uses racially aggravated prosecutions fairly selectively is only justifiable if it forms part of a more varied, holistic and vigorous policy of confronting expressive racism in different ways appropriate to the situation and the feelings of the victim. The criminal law is a blunt instrument for changing social attitudes but it is also a declaration of standards that forces recognition of wrongs that might otherwise be ignored. Nevertheless, preventitive measures, such as proactive work with perpetrators, deserve to receive the bulk of attention, rather than the reliance on prosecutions to transform behaviour.

Notes

1   See, for example, Lord Falconer on 12 February 1998, Hansard, Lords, vol. 585 col. 1270.

2   'An offence is racially or religiously aggravated', as amended by the Anti-Terrorism, Crime and Security Act 2001, section 39.

References

Home Office (2000), *Statistics on Race and the Criminal Justice System*, London: Home Office.

Iganski, P. (1999), 'Why make hate a crime?', *Critical Social Policy*, vol. 19, no. 3, 385–94.

—— (2001), 'Hate crimes hurt more', *American Behavioral Scientist*, vol. 45, no. 4, 626–38.

Lawrence, F. M. (1999), *Punishing Hate: Bias Crimes under American Law*, Cambridge, MA: Harvard University Press.

Morsch, J. (1991), 'The problem of motive in hate crime: the argument against presumptions of racial motivation', *Journal of Criminal Law and Criminology*, vol. 82, no. 3, 659–89.

Sentencing Advisory Panel (2000), *Advice to the Court of Appeal—4. Racially Aggravated Offences*, London: Home Office Communication Directorate.

Tevuchis, N. (1991), *Mea Culpa: The Sociology of Apology*, Stanford, CA: Stanford University Press.

8

PUNISH CRIME, NOT THOUGHT CRIME

Jeff Jacoby

They were crimes that shocked the nation. On 7 June 1998, three white ex-convicts in Jasper, Texas chained a forty-nine-year-old black hitchhiker to the back of a pickup truck and dragged him down a rough rural road to his death, his mutilated body parts leaving a trail nearly three miles long.

Four months later, in Laramie, Wyoming, a young gay man was lured from a student bar, driven out of town, beaten with a blunt instrument until his skull collapsed, hog-tied to a fence, and left for dead.

The murders of James Byrd, Sr. and Matthew Shepard scandalized and horrified Americans. Each drew enormous media attention and each was promptly seized upon as proof of the need for more and stronger laws to punish 'hate crimes'. Violence that stems from bigotry and intolerance, it was said, is worse than other kinds of violence. In President Bill Clinton's words: 'Crimes that are motivated by hate really are fundamentally different and I believe should be treated differently under the law.'

It is an argument that has met with much success. By 1998 hate crime legislation—laws increasing the punishment for a given crime when the offender acted out of certain specified types of prejudice or bigotry—was in force in 41 of the 50 US states. Limited hate crime laws were in force at the federal level, too: the Hate Crimes Sentencing Enhancement Act and the Violence against Women Act, for example. In 2000 and 2001 the US Senate (although not the House of Representatives) voted to expand sharply the federal government's authority to prosecute crimes stemming from bias, and to reach not only crimes based on race, colour, religion or national origin, but those motivated by the victim's sexual orientation or disability as well.

Notwithstanding their popularity, hate crime laws are badly misguided. The assumptions on which they are based do not stand up to scrutiny. And their ultimate effect will be to cause more damage than they prevent.

Hate crime laws are grounded in the conviction that attacks motivated by bigotry are more damaging than attacks stemming from other motivations. Certainly it is bad to be beaten by an attacker because he wants your money, the advocates of these laws say, but it is worse to be beaten by an attacker because he hates people of your colour or religion or sexual orientation. And, since a worse crime deserves a worse punishment, it is appropriate to increase the penalties meted out for hate crimes.

But is the premise really true? *Is* bigotry a more reprehensible motive than greed? Than lust? Than ideology? Than a desire to humiliate? It is hardly obvious that a hit-man who murders for money or a serial killer who does it for a thrill poses less of a threat to society—and therefore deserves less of a punishment—than someone who murders out of prejudice.

Hate crime laws declare, in effect, that the blood of a man attacked by a bigot is redder than that of a man attacked by a sadist or a thief. But what is the case for saying so? Do the children of a man murdered because he was black grieve less than the children of a man murdered because he had $50 in his pocket? Does the victim suffer less? If James Byrd had been dragged to his death by three black men, would his murder have been any less monstrous? In a society dedicated to the ideal of 'equal justice under law'—the words are engraved over the entrance to the Supreme Court in Washington, DC—it is unjust and indecent for the statute books to enshrine a double standard that makes some victims more equal than others.

Typically, supporters of hate crime laws justify the added penalties by claiming that the attacks cause added harm. 'Hate crimes are a form of terrorism,' said Senator Edward Kennedy of Massachusetts at a legislative hearing in 1998. 'They have a psychological and emotional impact which extends far beyond the victim. They threaten the entire community, and undermine the ideals on which the nation was founded.' Professor Kent Greenawalt of the Columbia University Law School makes a similar point: 'Such crimes can frighten and humiliate other members of the community; they can also reinforce social divisions and hatred.'

These observations are true, of course. But they are true of all violent crime. Every murder, every rape, every mugging victimizes more people than just the victim him/herself. That is one reason criminal prosecutions are always conducted in the name of the citizenry: *People* v. *Gacy, United States* v. *McVeigh, Commonwealth* v. *O'Neill.*

No reasonable person would deny that a violent crime committed against a member of a minority group can strike terror in the hearts of other members of that group. But non-hate crimes can do so as well. The kidnapping and murder of a child, the rape of a jogger in a public park, a drive-by gang shooting, the mugging of an elderly woman: don't these too 'have a psychological and emotional impact which extends far beyond the victim' to 'threaten the entire community'? It is not easy to see why the fear and menace felt by one segment of society—Jews, say, or Blacks—warrant the imposition of an extra-severe sentence while the fear and menace felt by another segment—senior citizens or residents of public housing or parents—don't.

Hate crime laws create an indefensible double standard. There is no way around it: a statute that imposes harsher penalties for hurting certain kinds of people proclaims by definition that hurting other kinds of people isn't quite as bad. Thugs who like to beat up Jews or Hispanics are on notice that the criminal code will increase their sentence if they are prosecuted and convicted. Thugs who like to beat up fat people—or socialists or businessmen or redheads or football fans—can do so with greater impunity. *Those* groups don't enjoy special protection.

Although most of the US states had enacted hate crime laws by 1998, two of those that hadn't were the ones where Byrd and Shepard were lynched: Texas and Wyoming. If they had, it was suggested, things would have been different. 'His death', editorialized the *New York Times* after Shepard was killed, 'makes clear the need for hate-crime laws to protect those who survive and punish those who attack others, whether fatally or not, just because of who they are'.

Likewise, Byrd's murder was cited as proof of the need for a tougher federal hate crime law. 'A strong response is clearly needed,' said Senator Kennedy not long after the killing in Jasper. To drive home the point, Byrd's daughter was brought to Washington to testify in the bill's favour.

But what difference could another hate crime law—state *or* federal—have possibly made? 'A strong response'? Of the three men who killed Byrd, two were sentenced to death and one is to spend the rest of his life behind bars. How much stronger a response did Kennedy have in mind? Shepard's killers, too, were sentenced to life imprisonment. One of them, Aaron McKinney, was facing a death sentence when Shepard's parents proposed a deal: two life sentences in exchange for a permanent gag order preventing McKinney from ever appealing the verdict or discussing the case in public. What could a hate crime law have done that the existing murder law didn't do?

'I'm convinced', Kennedy said at another hearing in 1999, that 'if Congress acted today, and President Clinton signed our bill tomorrow, we'd have fewer hate crimes in all the days that follow.' But this is specious. There is no state where prosecutors would ignore a monstrous violent crime or fail to demand a harsh punishment. Everything the murderers in Jasper and Laramie did—kidnapping, aggravated robbery, assault, murder—is already a crime in every US state and in every civilized country. Existing law provides harsh punishments. All that is necessary is to enforce the statutes already on the books.

The push for hate crime laws is fuelled by the belief that crimes based on hate have reached epidemic proportions. 'It has become nearly impossible to keep track of the shocking rise in brutal attacks directed against individuals *because* they are black, Latino, Asian, white, disabled, women, or gay,' write sociologists Jack Levin and Jack McDevitt in their 1993 book *Hate Crimes: The Rising Tide of Bigotry and Bloodshed.*

> *Almost daily, the newspapers report new and even more grotesque abominations ... As ugly as this situation is now, it is likely to worsen throughout the remainder of the decade and into the next century as the forces of bigotry continue to gain momentum.*

The same claim has been made repeatedly by politicians, scholars and various racial, religious and sexual activist organizations—and then amplified and re-broadcast by the media.

In the best book yet published on the subject—*Hate Crimes: Criminal Law and Identity Politics* (1998)—James B. Jacobs and Kimberly Potter round up an extraordinary collection of the alarmist rhetoric to which Americans have been exposed in recent years. Some sample headlines: A CANCER OF HATRED AFFLICTS AMERICA; RISE IN HATE CRIMES

SIGNALS ALARMING RESURGENCE OF BIGOTRY; BLACK-ON-WHITE HATE CRIMES RISING; DECADE ENDED IN BLAZE OF HATE; COMBATING HATE: CRIMES AGAINST MINORITIES ARE INCREASING ACROSS THE BOARD.

But dig into the statistics, and these turn out to be wild exaggerations. Hate 'crimes' are often not much more than incidents; in the FBI's official statistics, 'intimidation' is the most common offence, while the absolute number of violent bias crimes identified by the FBI is minuscule. Politicians, journalists and advocates find the notion of a hate crime 'epidemic' irresistible, perhaps because it is easier to denounce bigotry than to confront seriously violent crime in general. But the data are clear: of the roughly 20,000 homicides, 30,000 rapes, 150,000 robberies and half a million aggravated assaults for which police will make arrests in the United States this year, only the tiniest fraction would qualify as hate crimes. Nothing is gained by shining a spotlight on that fraction and eclipsing the rest.

One of the worst defects of hate crime laws is that they punish not just deeds, but opinions: not just what the criminal did, but what he believed. This amounts to an assault on freedom of speech and belief, and ought to have no part in the criminal justice system of a liberal democracy.

'There is no such crime as a crime of thought,' the renowned defence lawyer Clarence Darrow once said, 'there are only crimes of action'. In a free society, everyone is allowed to think bad thoughts and hold pernicious points of view. But contemporary hate crime laws turn those thoughts and points of view into crimes themselves. Certain states of mind, they declare, are so objectionable, so intolerable, that anyone who acts on them deserves especially severe punishment. Defenders of hate crime statutes argue that it is not the state of mind that is being punished, it is the crime it led to. But when the judge can send you to prison for an additional ten years because the aggravated assault you committed was motivated by your bigoted opinion of the victim, it is hard to reach any conclusion but the obvious one: your opinion has been criminalized.

'Thought crime', George Orwell called it in *Nineteen Eighty-Four*. A government that can punish you for your unorthodox thoughts about Blacks or Jews or homosexuals is that much closer to being able to punish you for your unorthodox thoughts about anything else. That is a prospect that should alarm any citizen who treasures his liberty.

In an age when citizens are under constant pressure to splinter into groups—to see themselves first and foremost as members of an aggrieved race, class or gender—the last thing they need are more laws emphasizing their differences and calling inordinate attention to bias and hatred. Hate crime laws further a deeply destructive trend: an insistence on casting violent offenders not merely as criminals who threaten society's well-being, but as various kinds of bigots: racists, sexists, gay-bashers, Jew-haters. This is profoundly wrong. The purpose of criminal law is not to protect Blacks from Whites, Jews from neo-Nazis, women from misogynists, gays from straights, or immigrants from nativists. It is to protect all of us from lawbreakers.

Every offence covered by a hate crime law was illegal to begin with. Each one could have been prosecuted under the existing criminal code. It may sound admirable to talk of 'preventing hate crimes' with new laws, but such laws prevent nothing except social unity. What they promote is balkanization, class warfare and identity politics.

Equal protection under law is the ideal of every democratic society. A government that takes that ideal seriously tells potential criminals that they will be punished fully and fairly, regardless of the identity of their victims. Hate crime laws, by contrast, declare that some victims are more deserving than others. That is a message no citizen should be willing to accept.

9

HATE CRIME: THE ORWELLIAN RESPONSE TO PREJUDICE

Melanie Phillips

In the wake of the September 2001 terrorist atrocities in the United States, the British government decided to assemble a package of anti-terrorist measures that would alter the balance between civil liberty and security. Most people would consider such a development appropriate and desirable in order to protect public safety in the face of further potential terrorist activity. And most people would probably agree that in the circumstances it was only reasonable that certain freedoms that were previously taken for granted must necessarily be compromised in order to safeguard life against such a potent threat.

However, one particular proposal threatened to exacerbate an already dangerous trend that was gaining ground before terror struck the West. The proposal was to introduce a law against incitement to religious hatred, an extension of the existing law against incitement to racial hatred. In addition, harsher penalties were being proposed for assaults that had a religious motive, a development of the relatively recent provision that had increased the penalties for assaults that had a racial motive.

These proposed extensions of the law were the government's response to pressure from the Muslim community, which was alarmed by the animosity that innocent Muslims were suffering as a result of the groundswell of popular feeling against Islamic fundamentalist terror. Certainly, the attacks on Muslims were deplorable and there was clearly a need to protect a community at risk of attack. However, the proposed law against incitement to religious hatred, as well as the stiffer penalties for racially motivated attacks, were not likely to increase anyone's physical safety. Rather than prevent threatening conduct, they would instead criminalize the wrong kind of speech or thought. The measures were in line with steady movement towards the introduction of hate crime statutes into English law, which has less to do with preventing harmful actions than extending identity politics and the victim culture into the field of crime and punishment.

Britain prides itself on being the cradle of free speech. But, in 2000, Alison Redmond-Bate was convicted of obstructing a police officer who stopped her preaching with her mother and another woman on the steps of Wakefield Cathedral. A crowd of more than a hundred had gathered and shouted 'bloody lock them up' and 'shut up' at the women. This wasn't the first time the preachers, members of an outspoken evangelical sect, had fallen foul of the law. The previous year, Redmond-Bate and her father had been found guilty of wilful obstruction after allegedly 'unsettling' the York crowd by warning them not to turn their backs on God.

It probably does get up a lot of people's noses to be told they're all sinners and will burn in hell. So what? Anyone who doesn't like it can walk away. The view that such preachers should be silenced because otherwise violence might erupt is over the top, to put it mildly. As Lord Justice Sedley observed when he allowed Redmond-Bate's appeal against her conviction, the idea that people would become violent from exposure to an in-your-face version of Thought for the Day was absurd. A bit of shouting from a crowd never harmed anybody. As for the suggestion that a speaker couldn't be accused of a breach of the peace as long as what she was saying was inoffensive, this was so dangerously wrongheaded that it inspired the judge to a ringing declaration. Free speech, he said, had to include 'the irritating, the contentious, the eccentric, the heretical, the unwelcome and the provocative', provided it didn't provoke violence.

Alas, Lord Justice Sedley is a voice from an already receding past. This is no longer a country that believes in robust free speech. It is far too terrified to give offence, the truly modern heresy. People who are foolish enough to assume that opinion is free may find themselves branded an enemy of the people.

George Staunton, a seventy-eight-year-old war veteran, thought that, while he was putting up posters for the UK Independence Party on a derelict wall, he would embellish their message by writing on the wall 'Don't forget the 1945 war' and 'Free speech for England'. Unfortunately, there was no free speech for Staunton as he was arrested and charged with racially aggravated criminal damage. Common sense finally penetrated the fog of the legal system and the case against him was dropped; but understandably he remained very upset. Causing damage is one thing; being a racist is another. As his solicitor, a civil liberties lawyer on Merseyside who knows a racist act when he sees one, pointed out, these remarks weren't racist at all. The police, he said, had been grossly irresponsible.

In fact, the attitude of the Merseyside police was ridiculous beyond belief. They boasted of having launched a 'dramatic, painstaking, dawn-till-dusk surveillance operation' against racist graffiti, whose prize catch was one seventy-eight-year-old male whose crime was to believe that Britain should be independent of Europe. This was Keystone Cops meet Big Brother after a course of racial awareness training. If this really is the face of the new racially sensitized, post–Stephen Lawrence police service, then heaven help the black community.

Of course, the Lawrence inquiry itself went down this same road when it recommended that it should be a crime to utter racist language in private. The fact that a tribunal of inquiry headed by a judge could have come up with a proposal of such totalitarian implications shows how dismayingly far we have already travelled. For, although this was ruled out by ministers, who could hardly have done otherwise given the barminess of the proposal, the government has nevertheless instituted crimes of racially motivated violence and racially aggravated damage. It has therefore, in effect, said that certain attitudes of mind are to be proscribed.

It did so because it wanted to give a signal to black people that it was serious about tackling the racism that undeniably exists. Yet a perfectly good law designed to prevent the consequences of racial hatred is rarely used. Strangely, law officers are reluctant to charge people with incitement to racial hatred, even though they may be distributing material that is not just offensive but dangerously inflammatory and intended to provoke real violence. Instead, the government apparently prefers people to be prosecuted for hurting others' feelings or for having the wrong opinion. This, of course, is likely to rebound in unexpected ways since freedom is indivisible and everyone is capable of being offended.

Andrew Wilson was fined £50 by Ipswich magistrates after police officers started checking why he was sitting in the street on a television set that he had been moving for a friend. Mr Wilson shouted: 'You white boys, you arrest black people for anything. You're white trash, you're only doing this because I'm a nigger. Leave me alone, you f***ing white trash, leave my black ass alone.' Hurling insults like this is certainly not admirable, but since when did it make anyone a criminal? Ever since the government passed a law against 'racially aggravated harassment'.

The irony, of course, is rich. Here was a law, passed to appease black people who think white society displays prejudice against them, being used against a black person for thinking that white police officers were displaying prejudice against him. This was extremely oppressive, but not for the reasons the black community is giving. They are outraged that any black person should be convicted of a racial offence, with the implication that only white people can be racist, a distorted view that merely illustrates the dismaying level of bitterness and sense of siege among black people. Passing laws to outlaw offensive thought is nevertheless the wrong way to tackle the alienation of black people, which has many justifiable causes. Instead of getting to grips with real issues of concern, which takes time and effort behind the scenes, the government has gone down the high-profile but counter-productive path of criminalizing thought itself. Wilson should never have been convicted for name-calling. Yet why was it worse for Wilson to have called the police 'white trash' than simply 'trash'?

Trying to eradicate 'hate' from the public realm is an American phenomenon that has crept up on us unawares. While the United States has balked at criminalizing hate speech itself, it has tried to eradicate the hate motive by increasing the penalties for crimes that are deemed to have a dimension of hatred. The position derives from the overriding injunction not to hurt anyone's feelings. Britain, however, is now going beyond increasing the penalties and is criminalizing speech itself. This is profoundly intolerant and illiberal. Freedom of speech is often difficult to take. People may say or write things with which we might vehemently disagree, or which we may find offensive. Tolerance, though, is all about allowing things to be said or done that we believe to be wrong—provided they don't cause harm. Freedom only lives if we disapprove of offensiveness, but defend it to the death.

The fixation with hate crime has helped to polarize American society quite viciously. Now this poisonous outgrowth of the rights culture has arrived in Britain. It was on egregious display in a dawn raid that netted more than 100 people who were arrested on charges of 'hate crimes', racist or homophobic abuse or attack, and domestic violence.

We used to have dawn raids by the drug squad. Now our daybreak derring-do is delivered by the hate squad, the Orwellian special units set up after the Macpherson report damned Britain as racist. In addition, the message has been appearing on cinema screens across London encouraging people to report hate crimes to their local police hate squads.

This development should cause us the greatest possible alarm. Of course people who hurt black people or homosexuals or members of their family should be brought to justice. But this goes far beyond that. These hate crimes are defined under the appalling and ludicrous maxim promulgated by Macpherson that a racist incident was one in which anyone involved thought it was racist. Now that this laughable subjectivity is being extended to other self-perceived victimizations, we are in the territory of thought crime.

Of course it is right for the police to encourage people to report offences. But why only hate crime? Why not burglary or grievous bodily harm? The police claim they are not saying hate crime is worse than other crime. But implicit in singling it out like this is the notion that motivation makes some crimes worse than others, that the pain and distress of being beaten to a pulp is not so bad if you are only a white heterosexual man.

All intimidation and assault is wrong and should be stopped. But the real purpose of categorizing hate crime is symbolic, in order to destroy prejudice and alter human nature.

This is as dangerous as it is implausible. These subjective and politicized definitions are capable of turning into a witch-hunt. Britain is one of the most tolerant and decent societies on earth. With young people being urged to inform on anyone who says something they think is unsayable, and a bureaucracy to make sure that we all toe the right ideological line, the stage is being set for a society of frightening intolerance and coercion.

And now, under the umbrella of the war against terror, it is proposed to create further thought crime offences. There are already plenty of laws that could be used to prevent harm to vulnerable groups, such as the law against incitement to violence. They are seldom used, however, because of a failure of political will. Creating a new law against religious hatred will do nothing to prevent attacks on Muslims. Instead, the danger is that it will be used to suppress legitimate comment and criticism.

An early example of the way it might be used occurred when Lady Thatcher expressed the view, a few weeks after the American atrocities, that Muslim clerics had not spoken out loudly enough against them. Whether or not one approved of what she said, she surely had a right to say it. Yet Lord Heseltine accused her of fomenting prejudice against Muslims, the editor of *Muslim News* demanded that her 'case' be sent to the Crown Prosecution Service and George Galloway MP said that, if the law against incitement to religious hatred had been in place, he would have insisted on her prosecution (while anti-western and anti-Israel hatred being preached in some mosques was an exercise in free speech).

.

Religion is a prime site of argument and disputation. A law against incitement to religious hatred has the potential to criminalize such discussion. It would be a way of extending the law of blasphemy to faiths other than Christianity and would finally deliver victory to those who wanted Salman Rushdie's *Satanic Verses* banned. Hate crime laws are an exercise in censorship. Ostensibly seeking to destroy prejudice, they hand power to self-designated victim groups to use against others. The harm that hate crime laws aim to prevent is already criminal. Prejudice and bigotry are subjective, and to criminalize them is not only oppressive but is likely to have a counter-productive effect.

10

HATE CRIMES HURT MORE, BUT SHOULD THEY BE MORE HARSHLY PUNISHED?

Paul Iganski

In his contribution to *The Hate Debate*, Jeff Jacoby argues that 'one of the worst defects of hate crime laws is that they punish not just deeds, but opinions—not just what the criminal did, but what he believed. This amounts', he continues, 'to an assault on freedom of speech and belief, and ought to have no part in the criminal justice system of a liberal democracy.' In a similar vein, Melanie Phillips suggests that hate crime laws are 'an Orwellian response to prejudice'.

However, against them, Frederick Lawrence argues: 'In a multi-ethnic society … we would expect bias-motivated crimes to receive some special treatment by the criminal law, to reflect the harm caused by the motivation underlying the crime.' Lawrence's argument is indicative of the way that the notion that hate crimes hurt more, and so deserve harsher punishment, has firmly entered into the discourse of defenders of hate crime laws (Iganski 2001).[1]

Is it possible to settle the debate between these opposing perspectives? One way might be to determine whether hate crimes do indeed hurt more. If they do, exactly what is the nature of the injuries inflicted? Do they amount to something other than revulsion at the offenders' motivating values or, in other words, the ideas in their heads?

Let's take physical injury first. Could it be that hate crime victims are more likely to sustain physical injuries than victims of the same, but otherwise motivated crimes? Some supporters of hate crime laws think so, suggesting that hate crimes are more likely to involve excessive violence and lead to hospital-ization than criminal assaults in general (cf. Levin 1999:15, Levin and McDevitt 1995).

The pain from physical injuries sustained by the victim of a hate-motivated attack obviously amounts to something other than being hurt by the offender's motivating values. But, think-ing logically, if physical injuries are to be used as a justification for treating hate crimes more seriously than the same parallel crimes, shouldn't it need to be the case that hate crimes usually, or even always, result in more severe injuries?

However, it would surely be remarkable if every violent crime resulted in greater injury when motivated by 'hate' than when otherwise motivated. Even if the majority of hate crimes inflict more serious injuries wouldn't it be unjust to punish more severely a perpetrator of a hate crime that didn't result in injury, by using the justification that *on average* hate crimes inflict more injuries? Data on the prosecution of racially aggra-vated offences in Britain show that offences involving physical violence against a person constitute a minority of prosecutions (Crown Prosecution Service 2001). Even if in each of those cases the victim was hurt more than they would have been in the same, but otherwise motivated assault, greater punishment is not justified in cases of such crimes that don't lead to physical injury.

Those hate crimes that do inflict greater physical injury obviously deserve to be punished more harshly. However, such crimes do not justify the creation of a whole class of punishment beyond the particular circumstances of any specific crime. Logically, crimes that inflict greater physical harms will be prosecuted at the appropriate level. That's why malicious wounding, for instance, is punished more severely than common assault.

Let's take a second type of injury. Victims of crime can also suffer emotional or psychological injury, as well as physical injury. Might the emotional consequences of hate crimes justify harsher punishment? In his essay in *The Hate Debate* Frederick Lawrence argues: 'Group-motivated crimes generally cause heightened psychological harm to victims over and above that caused by parallel crimes.' Recent research appears to support this argument. Gregory Herek and colleagues from the University of California at Davis compared a sample of lesbians and gay men who had been victims of hate crimes with a sample that had been victimized on other grounds than sexual orientation. They observed that the hate crime victims recorded higher scores on measures of depression, traumatic stress and anger (Herek, Gillis and Cogan 1999). However, whilst their data reveal that on average victims of hate crimes suffer more emotional harms, the evident variation in the scores indicates that not all victims experience harm to the same extent, and potentially some victims of non-bias crimes suffer greater emotional harm than some victims of hate crimes.

Understanding the emotional impact of hate crimes is essential for the provision of appropriate support for hate crime victims. However, as has just been argued in the case of physical injury, if psychological injuries are to be used as a justification for the law to treat hate crimes more seriously than the same parallel crimes, shouldn't it need to be the case that hate crimes usually, or even always, result in more severe psychological injuries? However, the research—such as that carried out by Herek and his colleagues—shows that they don't.

Let's take a third type of injury. Hate crimes arguably send out a terroristic message: violence, for instance, may constitute a threat of more violence (Weinstein 1992:8). In many cases the threat is real, as hate crime victims are more likely to be victimized repeatedly than victims of parallel crimes (cf. Bowling 1993). And, according to the US Bureau of Justice Assistance, 'a violent hate crime can act like a virus, quickly spreading feelings of terror and loathing across an entire community … violent hate crimes can create tides of retaliation and counter retaliation' (United States Bureau of Justice Assistance 1997:x).

Taking the potential for retaliation first, experimental research with college students in the United States has revealed that hate crimes are more likely to generate a desire for revenge than otherwise motivated crimes (Craig 1999). In addition, the Los Angeles riots following the beating of Rodney King and, in Britain, the more recent race riots in Oldham, Bradford and Burnley clearly demonstrate how hate crimes can stir up a community, especially where there are already simmering grievances. Parallel crimes don't have the same impact. We would not normally expect a riot to break out in response to a drunken assault outside a bar on a Saturday night.

However, justifying the more severe punishment of hate crimes by arguing that they are more serious because they can potentially provoke further crimes makes a very weak case. It amounts to justifying extra punishment of an offender because he had the misfortune to choose a victim for whom others are prepared to fight back by committing illegal acts of violence in return (Jacobs and Potter 1998:88).

Instead, the terror—or the fear of victimization—potentially generated by hate crimes makes a stronger claim for their greater punishment. In the Fourth National Survey of Ethnic Minorities, carried out in Britain in the mid-1990s, nearly one-quarter of black and Asian respondents reported being worried about being 'racially harassed'. Fourteen per cent of the respondents had taken measures to avoid potential harassment, ranging from going out less at night to avoiding particular pubs and other changes in leisure activity. More respondents in the survey were worried about being racially harassed than had actually experienced it in the previous year. This suggests that an incident of racial harassment in a neighbourhood, or elsewhere, can create an atmosphere of fear and anxiety even for those who haven't been personally victimized (Virdee 1997:284–5).

However, as already argued, justification of the punishment of hate crimes as a separate class of crimes needs to be supported by evidence that the impact of a hate crime usually goes above and beyond the impact of the same, but otherwise motivated crime. Unfortunately, the Fourth National Survey of Ethnic Minorities does not report on respondents' experiences of ordinary crime, that is, crimes not motivated by hate. So it is not possible to say conclusively that hate crimes terrorize communities more than other crimes (a burglary or a mugging in which an elderly person is victimized, for instance). All violent crimes potentially terrorize communities. More research is needed to show that hate crimes terrorize communities more, if the argument that they do is to be used to support hate crime laws.

There is a further type of harm that arguably provides the strongest support for the notion that hate crimes hurt more. Whilst all types of crime might be offensive to the majority of law-abiding citizens, crimes motivated by hate are arguably more offensive to society than those motivated by other reasons. As Frederick Lawrence argues: 'Such crimes violate not only society's general concern for the security of its members and their property but also the shared values of equality among its citizens, and racial and religious harmony in a multicultural society.' Hate crimes then offend societal norms, or the collective moral code; and a dominant norm in diverse multicultural societies is a respect for that diversity. Hate crime offenders are entitled to their reservations and opinions about living with diversity. However, when they act on those opinions and commit crimes motivated by bigotry, they offend values that are fundamental to civil society. That's what hurts. But it doesn't hurt everybody, as evidenced by the scale of the problem of hate crimes and the number of people who carry them out.

Advocating the more severe punishment of hate crimes—compared with parallel crimes—on the grounds that they offend societal values can amount to nothing other than advocating punishment of the values of the offender. Should supporters of hate crime laws then stand by their principles and honestly declare that their objective is to punish offenders for their bad values, values incongruent with civil society? Perhaps they should. Would that concede victory in the debate to opponents of hate crime laws who argue that they punish thought and opinion? Yes, it would, but only partially. It is not the thought alone that is being punished: it is the thought in the context of the criminal act.

Opponents of hate crime laws argue that the laws are illegitimate because they take values into account in determining punishment. But there is a flaw in their argument. It is not unusual for the criminal law to use an offender's motivating values to determine the seriousness of the offence and the appropriate punishment (Hare 1997). Self-defence, for instance, is seen as a mitigating factor with regard to culpability for a crime, even though the consequences of the crime might be identical to the same offence committed out of malice. Good—or normatively desirable—values are rewarded by courts; bad values are punished (Kahan 2001). And there is no sign yet that the Orwellian nightmare is about to occur. There is no inconsistency, therefore, in punishing hate crime offenders more than others for their motivating values.

However, a troublesome issue remains. If hate crime offenders are to be more severely punished—than offenders in parallel crimes—for offending societal norms, or for any other harms they inflict, shouldn't justice require that they are culpable for the consequences of their actions? But do the perpetrators always intend the injuries they cause?

The limited research evidence that there is on offender motivations in hate crimes suggests that many offenders may not intend all of the harm they inflict. Jack Levin and Jack McDevitt, from Boston's Northeastern University, carried out a much-cited analysis of hate crimes recorded by the Boston Police Department. They report that the most common (58 per cent) type of hate crime was 'committed by groups of offenders simply for the thrill or excitement' (Levin and McDevitt 1995). 'Surprisingly', they go on to claim, 'the offenders in thrill hate crimes are not particularly committed to prejudice. They frequently go along to please or be accepted by their friends' (1995:7).[2]

It is feasible that the actions of thrill-seekers and offenders motivated by peer group dynamics will generate waves of terror and fear, and also potentially offend many people's values. However, are such offenders culpable for all of the consequences of their crimes? It is likely that they may not have intended, or anticipated, any consequences beyond the impact upon their immediate victims. Might their lack of intent therefore mitigate their guilt in the same way that a person whose actions negligently result in the death of another is deemed guilty of a less serious offence than the person who intends to kill?

Hate crimes are often seen as message crimes, conveying the bigotry of the perpetrator to the victim. When an offender is consciously acting out their bigotry to a violent conclusion, the criminal law, and the courts, provide an appropriate way of sending a message back: such behaviour will not be tolerated in civil society. By punishing such offenders the law has an important symbolic value. This was clearly the intent of supporters of the establishment of racially aggravated offences in Britain (Iganski 1999).

However, prosecution of hate crime offenders also needs to be sensitive to the context of the crime, and sensitive to the seriousness of the crime. In cases in which offenders are articulating and mirroring the prejudices of those around them, rather than instrumentally administering bigotry, a more holistic intervention might be more appropriate than recourse to the courts. In such cases we might think more about perpetrator communities than individual perpetrators (Sibbitt 1997). As Larry Ray and David Smith argue in their essay in *The Hate Debate*, focusing on the motives of individual perpetrators runs the risk of overlooking the cultural and societal context of their crimes, and especially the way that violence is used as a social resource. As Jack Levin observes in his essay: 'It would be comforting if we were able to characterize hate and prejudice as deviant, irrational and pathological behaviour', but 'it is part of the culture—the way of life—of the society in which it exists ...' However, we have yet to understand adequately how best to deal with so-called 'hate crime' offenders in the context of the cultural values that fuel their crimes.

Notes

1   The notion that hate crimes hurt more has also been highly influential, as greater punishment for greater harm was accepted by Chief Justice Rehnquist, writing for the majority in *Wisconsin* v. *Mitchell* (113 S. Ct. at 2201 [1993]), the landmark case that settled the constitutional challenge to hate crime legislation in the United States. According to Rehnquist: 'the Wisconsin statute singles out for enhancement bias-inspired conduct because this conduct is thought to inflict greater individual than societal harm. For example, according to the State and its amici, bias motivated crimes are more likely to provoke retaliatory crimes, inflict distinct emotional harms on their victims, and incite community unrest. The State's desire to redress these perceived harms provides an adequate explanation for its penalty-enhancement provisions over and above mere disagreement with offenders' beliefs and biases.'

2   Offenders were classified in a similar way in a recent survey of students at six community colleges in Northern California in which 10 per cent of respondents admitted physical violence or threats against presumed

homosexuals, and 24 per cent reported anti-gay name-calling. According to Karen Franklin, two of the motivations behind incidents, 'Thrill Seeking and Peer Dynamics, both stem from adolescent developmental needs. *Thrill Seekers* commit assaults to alleviate boredom, to have fun and excitement, and to feel strong. *Peer Dynamics* assailants commit assaults in order to prove their toughness and heterosexuality to friends. Both Thrill Seekers and Peer Dynamics assailants minimise their personal antagonism toward homosexuals, and either blame their friends for assaults or minimise the level of harm done' (Franklin 2000).

References

Bowling, B. (1993), 'Racial harassment and the process of victimization', *British Journal of Criminology*, vol. 33, no. 2, 231–49.

Craig, K. M. (1999), 'Retaliation, fear, or rage. An investigation of African American and White reactions to racist hate crimes', *Journal of Interpersonal Violence*, vol. 14, no. 2, 138–51.

Crown Prosecution Service (2001), *Racist Incident Monitoring Annual Report 1999–2000*, London: Crown Prosecution Service.

Franklin, K. (2000), 'Antigay behaviors by young adults: prevalence, patterns and motivators in a noncriminal population', *Journal of Interpersonal Violence*, vol. 15, no. 4, 339–62.

Hare, I. (1997), 'Legislating against hate: the legal response to bias crime', *Oxford Journal of Legal Studies*, vol. 17, no. 3, 415–39.

Herek, G. M., J. R. Gillis and J. C. Cogan (1999), 'Psychological sequelae of hate-crime victimization among lesbian, gay, and bisexual adults', *Journal of Consulting and Clinical Psychology*, vol. 67, no. 6, 945–51.

Iganski, P. (1999), 'Why make hate a crime?', *Critical Social Policy*, vol. 19, no. 3, 385–94.

———— (2001), 'Hate crimes hurt more', *American Behavioral Scientist*, vol. 45, no. 4, 626–38.

Jacobs, J. B. and K. A. Potter (1998), *Hate Crimes. Criminal Law and Identity Politics*, New York: Oxford University Press.

Kahan, D. M. (2001), 'Two liberal fallacies in the hate crimes debate', *Law and Philosophy*, vol. 20, 175–93.

Levin, B. (1999), 'Hate crimes. Worse by definition', *Journal of Contemporary Criminal Justice*, vol. 15, no. 1, 6–21.

Levin, J. and J. McDevitt (1995), 'Landmark study reveals hate crimes vary significantly by offender motivation', *Klanwatch Intelligence Report*, August, Montgomery, AL: Southern Poverty Law Center.

Sibbitt, R. (1997), *The Perpetrators of Racial Harassment and Racial Violence*, Home Office Research Study 176, London: Home Office.

United States Bureau of Justice Assistance (1997), *A Policymaker's Guide to Hate Crimes*, Washington, DC: US Department of Justice, Bureau of Justice Assistance.

Virdee, V. (1997), 'Racial harassment', in T. Modood, R. Berthoud, J. Lakey, J. Nazroo, P. Smith, S. Virdee and S. Beishon (eds), *Ethnic Minorities in Britain. Diversity and Disadvantage*, London: Policy Studies Institute.

Weinstein, J. (1992), 'First Amendment challenges to hate crime legislation: where's the speech?', *Criminal Justice Ethics*, vol. 11, no. 2, 6–20.